Teaching Children to Paint

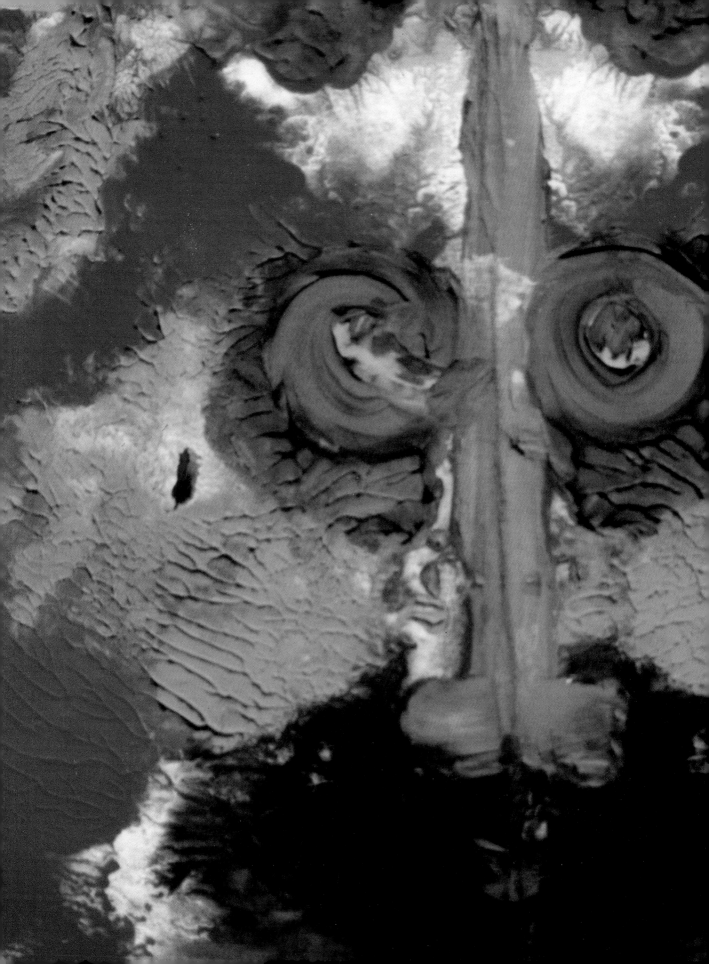

Teaching Children to Paint

Written by Karla Cikánová

CRAFTSMAN HOUSE

This edition first published in 1993 by Craftsman House BVI Ltd., Tortola, BVI
Distributed in Australia by Craftsman House,
20 Barcoo Street,
East Roseville, NSW 2069, Australia

Distributed internationally through the following offices:

USA
STBS Ltd.
PO Box 786
Cooper Station
New York
NY 10276

UK
STBS Ltd.
5th Floor, Reading Bridge House
Reading Bridge Approach
Reading RGI 8PP
England

ASIA
STBS (Singapore) Pte Ltd.
No. 25 Tannery Road
Singapore 1334
Republic of Singapore

ISBN 976 8097 39 6

Written by Karla Cikánová
Translated by Alena Linhartová
Illustrations by children from the Primary School,
Londýnská Street, Prague
Instructive drawings by Michal Skalník
Instructive photographs by Jindřich Richter
Photographs in Mini-galleries by Pavel Brunclík (46 C, 110 A,
111 C), Blanka Chocholová (124 A), Karla Cikánková (22 B,
23 C, D, 34 C, 46 D, 87 D, 98 A, 110 B), Dušan Dukát (99 C),
Ivan Kafka (47 F), Bohumil Landisch (34 A, 86 A), Anna
Rauerová (124 B, D), Jindřich Richter (60 A, B), Pavel
Šamšula (22 A, 46 A, B, 74 C, D, 99 D), Martin Setvák (74 A,
B, 75 E, F, G), Pavel Štecha (35 D, 61 C, 125 C), Gabriel
Urbánek (86 B), Petr Znamenaný (47 E, 87 C)
Graphic design by Vladimír Rocman and Ludmila Zapletalová

Printed in the Czech Republic
1/99/44/51-01

Contents

Preface

What the children said about colours:

'If at first I could only see in black and white or grey and then was suddenly able to see in colour I would be very happy and turn into a butterfly so that I could touch all those colours properly.' . . . 'I always feel like touching colours and then painting my face using them' . . . 'I think I would enjoy most eating the colour pink because it is the colour of watermelon' . . . 'Why did I blacken that picture at the end? Because I dreamt it all at night.' . . . 'A yellow sun always turns green in my pictures when a blue cloud passes over it.' . . . 'Detective stories are violet, grey and at the end yellow.' . . . 'I like wearing this T-shirt because I have painted it with blueberries myself.' . . . 'I stuck my picture out in the rain and immediately it looked much better.' . . . 'Mum laughed that I had painted her in rosy colours and said that when she sometimes looked at me she saw black.' . . . 'John painted a self-portrait in such a way that he first coloured his face and then covered it in paper.' . . . 'When I cry it seems that black tears stream down my face.'

Hearing sounds is not the same as knowing how to listen to music. Likewise, a sensitive perception of the world of colours is a special skill. Colour vision really is a magnificent gift, as without it we would only be able to see in black and white or grey. We would give each other grey roses on birthdays, and we would eat grey oranges. However, many of us only appreciate this invaluable gift of colour vision when angry colours shout at us and try to outbid one another as if they were trinkets and trifles on a market stall. We should, in fact, be deeply concerned by a lack of colour sensitivity, as we would undoubtedly be if we had an untreated illness. We should run quickly into the nearest wood and look there for dozens of shades of green. Or else go to a gallery and conduct a quiet dialogue with the heavenly blues in Marc Chagall's pictures. However, the most effective remedy might be the one offered by children — a return to the world as seen through their eyes, as if 'for the very first time'.

Talk to children about the magnificent world of colours. Such talk is mutually beneficial and deepens our conscious perception. It also provides us with an exceptional opportunity to arouse and develop children's ability to perceive the world around them in all its diversity and the range of colour often hidden under a seemingly inconspicuous surface. And if, by chance, when working with children we regret that as adults we may not challenge the world of colour in active painting, we can at least console ourselves with what Christian Morgenstern said: 'Even perception itself represents creativity.'

This second volume of painting activities for eight- to twelve-year-old children is devoted to creative expression using colour. It is written for adults who are involved with the art education of children, namely art teachers, educationalists and parents.

This publication offers children a stimulus for enjoyable encounters with colour. The introductory chapters present specific suggestions for emotive and imaginative painting and colour collages. Later chapters deal with topics which lead to the more conscious application of colour relationships. Creative activities are based on a gradual introduction to the basics of colour classification. Children attempt to tackle topics according to a pre-determined palette of warm and cold colours. They also use the contrasts of light and saturation: colour accent.

Topics are freely linked to painting done from life or through the imagination. The possibilities of colour expressed through toy design and interior decoration in the environment are also explored.

Throughout the book the text itself and picture captions recommend and reinforce technical approaches to individual topics (such as using a brush or a spatula; the procedures recommended for glazing and paste painting; embedding colours; monotypes; spraying and covering; varieties of colour collages). At the same time suitable topics are defined for younger children, the eight- to ten-year-old range, and for older children, the eleven- to twelve-year-old range.

Each chapter concludes with a two-page Mini-gallery. These Mini-galleries remind us of unusual encounters with colour. They include photographs of the natural world and creative photography and also works of art in which colour is the fundamental form of expression.

All the children's illustrations in this book were produced under the direct supervision of the author, an art teacher in a Prague primary school.

Karla Cikánová

1

1

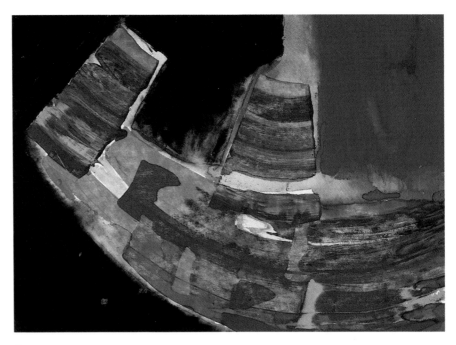

2

1 *Random Imprints* made with tin lids and crushed pieces of paper soaked in tempera paints create simple colour games. These games are popular with both younger and older children. They can discover interesting colour groups and surfaces using a paper viewfinder.

2 *What a Palette Knife Can Do*. A ten-year-old boy squeezed tempera paints directly from a tube onto paper and then spread and mixed them together with the firm movement of a palette knife (or a plastic strip). He painted the background in dark colours.

Unusual Encounters with Colours

Looking for opportunities. Coloured bottles. Colour collages and de-collages. Rain paintings. Colour windmills — monotypes. Expressions through brush and spatula.

The pleasure of encountering colour does not only arise when one paints on a sheet of paper. The world is filled with coloured objects which children can assemble or transfer. Unusual encounters with colour can be achieved while playing.

An opportunity offers itself when children go swimming in the countryside in summer. They can create huge flat figures or fantastic coloured animals using their own coloured T-shirts, skirts, hats, towels and rugs. If children stuff T-shirts and form shapes with belts, they can create three-dimensional animals.

3 a

If children miss colours on a dull winter's day they can paint a snowman with water paints or hang coloured paper leaves or ribbons on the branches of a leafless tree.

Children may prefer coloured objects of a more permanent nature. 'Coloured jars' are rather interesting if plastic transparent bottles are used. Children can put them on a windowsill so that

3 a, b *Coloured Bottles* are in fa rainbow marbles, buttons, strir beads and even coloured pebbl placed in water or lightly coloured ir Children put the bottles on a windows so that their colours could be reveale On some bottles they put an advertis ment label bearing a made-up nam and description.

b

A Game with Differently Coloured Peelings from Apples, Oranges and Lemons is an example of simple in. Strips of peel can be variously displayed on a surface, or three-dimensional structures of peel and toothpicks stuck into an apple can be created. Similarly, coloured autumn leaves, buttons or rows of beads can be used. Children gain pleasure and satisfaction from the colour combinations and variations which they create.

4

they catch the light. Even the simple task of pouring coloured ink slowly into a bottle filled with water can bring a lot of pleasure. Children feel like alchemists and will compete with each other as to how many beautifully coloured 'drinks' they can create using drawing ink and inks. One can also suggest inserting smaller bottles containing coloured water into larger bottles. Or they could

5

5 *What is Hidden Under Wallpaper?* More and more layers of differently coloured wallpaper. An older boy made this de-collage. The Instructional Illustration above shows how he proceeded. Remind children that properly diluted glue is essential for success, otherwise the layers of coloured papers may dry out before being torn off.

13

6   **7**

6 *The Sun Amongst Trees.* Th
picture was made accidentally a
a coloured 'surprise' while sprayin
colours through paper templates an
other objects.

7 *A Fisherman's Hut with Fishir
Nets Drying.* This picture, too, was cre
ated accidentally, by spraying crec
sote, inks and non-toxic textile dye. I
creator, a boy, fixed paper to a slopin
board. He pinned several tiny objects
such as pieces of string, torn-up bits o
paper and thin netting, onto the pape
He then sprayed everything with co
our. When the colour dried he move
the objects and, using a paint gun, h
sprayed the paper with a different co
our (below). He repeated this proces
several times. Finally, he titled the pic
ture according to what it reminde
him of.

put in beads or marbles, coloured leaves or apple peel, strips of coloured cellophane or transparent bags containing coloured water. If children shake a sealed bottle the colour composition will change.

Children can use old magazines to play another game. They tear out interesting coloured surfaces and sort them into shades of blue, red, green, grey and black. By sorting paper surfaces according to their colour children have all the materials which they

8

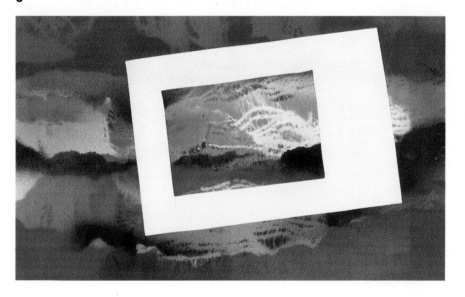

8 *Discovering the Countryside* usinç
a viewfinder. Children are keen to dis
cover smaller designs and surfaces
which are interesting from the point o
colour or shape on their sprayed 'sur
prises'. They choose an appropriate
title for these.

14

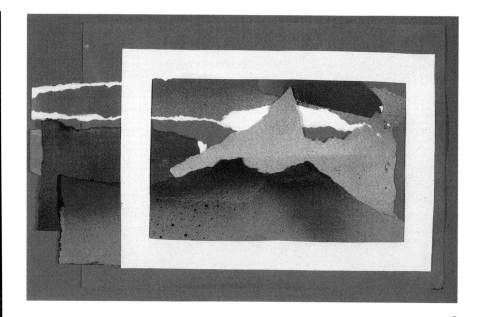

9 *A Free Collage of the Countryside* using pieces of paper left over from previous works and a paint gun (see also below). The children insert pieces of paper torn off lengthwise under a frame, and then move them around freely. When they are happy with the colour and shape of their composition they glue them partially or completely to a larger white or coloured sheet of paper.

need to play. Graphic designers also employ pre-coloured or overprinted sheets of paper to create a picture. Some children might play a game in which they assemble coloured areas. They glue coloured surfaces randomly and in several layers onto the surface of A-4 paper, using a waterbased glue. Their compositions can but do not have to have a definite purpose in mind. They can first work with differently shaded blue pieces, on top of these put red pieces and finally other coloured papers. A collage is finished whenever the children are happy with their own colour composition.

Children can also try the opposite, the so-called de-collage. Children swap the wet collages amongst themselves and tear off parts of piled-up areas. This results in the creation of variations — new coloured 'surprises' as wet layers peel off differently. Children can also glue peeled-off pieces onto a different area on their sheet of paper. The finished works may remind them of an old advertising hoarding.

Spraying colours with a spray gun through a template can result in striking coloured 'surprises'. Children move around and spray 'templates' made of various materials, such as frayed sackcloth, odd pieces of paper, lengths of string, and even stones and leaves. The shapes which result from certain areas being covered to form outlines may remind children of fantastic countries or animals or their movements. Children might discover similar coloured 'surprises' on a visit to a painter's workshop. These 'surprises' also occur by chance when working with colour.

10

Pictures 6 and 7 show the sort of template (i.e. shape and material) children can use to spray onto a sheet of paper.

It would be a pity not to make use of previously created work such as coloured areas. Encourage children to tear the sprayed work, which they do not want to keep, into interesting coloured surfaces. They can do the same with previously used 'templates'.

11

12

12 *A Water-Printed Monotype.* Icicles, plants or a rippled water surface can be created by dragging wet paper across a sheet of glass with paints spread on its surface. Illustrators and animators use similarly created surfaces as colour supplements to their pictures.

13 *A Rotated Monotype* created between two sheets of glass (or two sheets of paper) shows how colours blend with circular movement. Children can observe a similar colour effect when riding on a fast-moving merry-go-round.

We then provide viewfinders. These are oblong frames cut out of paper to resemble picture frames. Children insert and exchange torn-off coloured papers underneath the frame. It is unnecessary to glue collages as they can help to develop sensitivity with regard to coloured compositions through rapid exchanges. Even painters when wandering through the countryside occasionally use an ob-

13

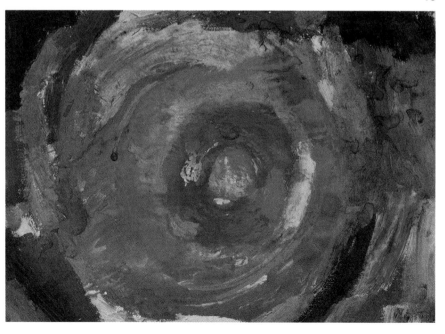

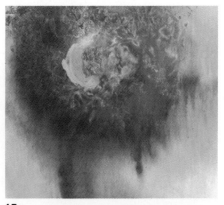

15

14

16

14—16 *What the Rain Can Pair*
Younger children tried this activit
They observed the effect of raindrop
flowing down at an angle on pap
painted with tempera paints. Childre
gave these pictures the followin
names — A Mysterious Rock, How th
Sun Cries, Islands in the Sea. Yo
children will no doubt be able to recog
nise which picture is which.

long viewfinder. They position it in front of their eyes and try to arrange in the frame the colours and shapes in nature which might inspire them to paint. Pictures 8 and 9 show how children worked with similar viewfinders.

We have so far only dealt with colour enounters and changes. Later activities will involve games with colours which reflect the children's willingness and eagerness to confront colour material directly. We refer to prints — the so-called monotypes. A monotype is a single print taken from a freshly painted block. Children can paint their own hands with thick tempera paint and make prints on paper. They can also imprint on wet paper a piece of cloth used to wash a palette or make an impression of the palette itself. Even painters and designers sometimes use their fingers, pieces of cloth or a palette knife to paint. Children can visually demonstrate the making of a monotype using two transparent sheets of glass between which tempera paints are squeezed and spread.

When working with colours it is important to realise the import-

7 *Blue and Red Colours.* An older boy squeezed red and blue colours directly out of tempera tubes. He then carefully planned movements with a palette knife so that colours would blend in some places and remain isolated in others.

17

8 *A Test of All My Tempera Paints.* This picture was made using several palette knives. The child first practised holding the knives correctly so that they stayed flexible and adhered closely to the paper when moved below). Paints were positioned at the top of the paper and spread by the knives towards the bottom. The knives had to be kept clean in order to achieve sharp results.

ance of water in diluting watercolours and tempera paints. If more water is added paints disperse and lose colour, which results in softer outlines and areas becoming mysterious. Pictures 14,15, and 16 were in fact created by rain. Thick tempera paints on a sheet of paper positioned at an angle were exposed to heavy rain.

When painting children will notice that colours squeezed thickly

18

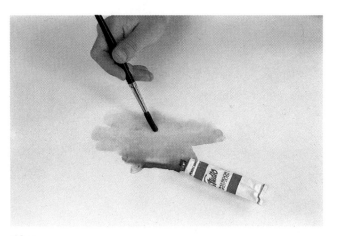

19 a   **b**

out of a tube keep their original rich colouring and the resulting fur-rowed and uneven surface creates an interesting texture. It is possible to sculpt such textures. Children require only a few plastic strips to spread and knead paints. Pictures 2,17 and 18 show how to use these strips.

It is worth mentioning that Gustav Courbet (1819—77) spread colours with a knife and that Vincent van Gogh (1853—90), when painting his windswept and glowing landscapes, squeezed colours onto the canvas directly from the tube.

Some basic instructions on the painting procedures shown in Picture 19:
a) Washing out a rich and thick tempera paint using a round brush. It is import-ant to have a cloth at hand, not too wet, to wipe the brush. Surplus water can be removed from paper using a half-dry brush.

19 *Instructions on Painting Proce-dures:*
a) washing out
b) paste painting
c) using a paper template
d) spreading pastels
e) washing out pastels
 f) waxed pastels do not absorb water

c

d

e

b) Children can master the various degrees of rich and thick colour, typical of paste painting, if they use a hard flat brush or a knife. Brushstrokes are easily recognisable.

c) Painting with a flat brush across the edge of a paper template can be used to achieve a sharp edge, i.e. colour fringing. Obviously the colour area under the template must already be dry.

d) Thick dry pastels or chalks can be used for colour linear drawings and for painting. Children first colour the surface using chalks and then decide which areas they will rub with their fingers or a duster made of rolled soft paper.

e) Dry pastels or chalks can be washed out with water or children can paint with them directly onto a wet surface.

f) Note that waxed pastels do not absorb water, so if children paint over waxed pastels with a thinner colour, then the pastel will show through on the sufrace.

f

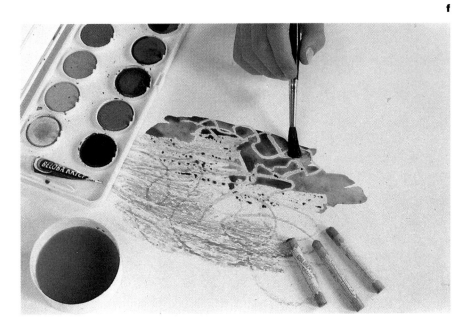

A *The Scratched Banister* has experienced rough handling. The picture reminded the children of burning fire, the bark of an exotic tree or part of a snake's body.

B *The Leaves of a Tropical Plant* resemble the Scratched Banister in colour. The arrangement of the leaves' colours corresponds to their symmetrical structure along the axis.

A

B

C *The Red Eyes* were created quite by chance from two transparent glass bowls used to observe how paints intermingled on their bases. When the children put the bowls on the windowsill to dry, with an old iron as a weight, it looked as if a fairy tale dragon was peeping into the room.

D *Painted Pebbles* can be used for a game. Can the children guess how many red pebbles there are?

C

D

2

21

20 *An Enchanted Countryside.* An older boy created this collage using magazine illustrations which he coloured with felt-tip pens. Several mysterious black castles with a coloured background suggest that the whole countryside is enchanted. The black colour casts a spell on every living thing. Other colours seem to be in a deep sleep, waiting, as if in a fairy tale, for someone to come and free them from a nightmare.

21 *A Fantastic Dream-like Countryside* was created by embedding colours on a wet surface. The colours blend and the picture is reminiscent of a quickly forgotten dream. The girl creator provided an accompanying commentary which reads like a fairy tale: 'I painted a house on the bank of a river where Fan and his sister Tazia live. In the evening they turn into black and white swans. Then they fly to visit the man in the Moon. Children can only see Fan and Tazia in their dreams.

Pictures of Emotions and Moods

Subjective perception of colours; paintings of fairy lands and the land of dreams. Portraits of people and pictures of animals. How to depict the emotions and moods revealed during children's games. Painting sensual experience.

Certain colours and colour combinations can, in their own right, recall notions of something familiar in nature or in the world of objects (green: grass; red: a roof). Colours can also revive memories of a strong subjective experience, such as a crimson sky. The subjective notion of colour is interesting and complex. Colours can be associated with the days of the week; with people we know; with activities; moods; or even sounds and smells. This colour perception of taste, smell, and sound can be explained by the fact that the sensory centres are situated close to one another in the brain where their interconnection has been well established.

We can test how rich and varied this seemingly unusual associ-

22

23

ation of colours is in a game which might inspire children to further activities. Children will need watercolours, several brushes and a glass of water. We then distribute to the children a set of small white cards which bear on their bottom edge individual words, such as mother, father, grandparents, Sunday, Monday, birthday, crying, laughter, anger, sour, bitter, sweet. Children paint onto the card one or at the most two colours which they associate with the respective word. Pastel pinks and light blue colours are often associated with the word 'mother'; whereas 'grandmother' is usually associated with golden-brown colours. If several children participate in the game, it is possible to compare card colours for 'mother', 'Sunday' or 'pleasure'.

It is interesting to hear the reasons children give for selecting one colour rather than another. Children assign colour to fairy tale characters according to what these represent — good, evil, kindness, defencelessness, slyness. When painting portraits of characters and animals from fairy tales and legends, children can use

22 *The Good Magician*. A younger child added red, orange and yellow colours to illuminate a face in this portrait of 'Goodness'. The secret magic properties of 'Goodness' are represented by blue and black colours in the unlit parts of the face. The creator of this picture used a black and white photograph of George Bernard Shaw as a model for an older bearded face. The child freely interpreted the novelist's face in tempera paints on a large sheet of paper.

23 *The Bad Wizard*. This face is a symbol of evil, cunning and hostility. The artist used yellow tempera paints combined with black and greys to correspond to the character described. The painting is executed boldly with incisive strokes of a broad brush. The eyes, which project malice and make one shudder, have been made very prominent.

26

24 *Man and the Countryside.* An older boy created this collage. He combined landscapes and a portrait. He glued everything down and then produced an even tone with thinner colours. He wrote that the picture showed an ecologist who wondered how to save threatened rivers and forests. Similarly, we can inspire other colour associations between a person's portrait and his or her immediate environment and activities, such as a gardener and his garden; a man and his car; a writer and her books. Younger children like to associate fairy tale portraits with collages of the countryside, such as a king and his castle, a water sprite and its lake.

24

their individual perception of colours. It is important to encourage children to talk about their notions of colour in an instructional discussion prior to painting. We can learn that a dragon's lair consists of poisonous and wicked colours, which in their own right 'terrify and threaten'; that a castle with a bewitched princess is 'as if in a fog, dreary and dull'. By the same token children are able to find colours for the tender daydreaming of princesses; the clowning of jesters; the dancing of sprites and fairies.

25

25 *A Magic Fish Which May Grant Three Wishes or a Happy Christmas Carp Which is Not Going to be Killed and Eaten.* This painting by an eight-year-old child shows that in a fairy tale a magic creature can symbolise Good. A magic creature can also symbolise Evil — children would undoubtedly use different colours to paint a fearsome dragon or a big bad wolf. Find out how many good and evil fairy tale characters the children know.

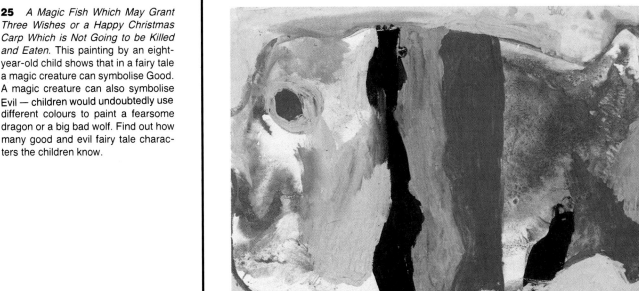

26

27

Older children can express their subjective colour perception with regard to their reading. We can introduce a topic 'My Bookcase at Home' in an instructional talk. In this talk we can find out which literary genre children like most and with what colour they associate it. They usually associate green colours with travelogues; brown and sunny yellow colours with historical novels; and mysterious compositions of violet colours contrasted with yellow for detective stories and science fiction. Pictures 26 and 27 show us that this attempt to express their favourite reading in colour represents a spontaneous transition from concrete fairy tale painting to more abstract painting expressed through simple lines, shapes and colours or a definite sign of what is seemingly invisible.

Concrete and abstract painting includes the expression of moods (e.g. happiness), characteristic features (e.g. diligence) and states (e.g. old age). Younger children can be asked to paint a wide-brimmed hat which would put them in a good mood, and

26 *I Like Reading Funny Stories*. In this picture the children painted their own bookcases using a palette knife. They associated their favourite reading genre, in this case funny travelogues and nature books depicted as a cluster of book spines, with a chosen colour.

27 *My Bookcase*. A girl explained her choice of colours with reference to her poetry reading. First, she spread colours on a wet surface using a palette knife, then, using a soft brush dipped in water, she thinned the colour blocks into backgrounds.

28

28 *Fear.* An example of emotional abstract painting. The artist added this explanation to his picture: 'Fear of something is somehow sneaking up on you; it attacks you suddenly, so that you feel hot and then frozen a second later; you cower and start shivering. Fear is like a snake in poisonous crude colours which are invisible in the dark.'

28

whisk them high up into the sky. It is very important to have an instructional talk before the children attempt an abstract expression of a mood using only colours, lines and shapes. Children like to talk in similes: 'It is like . . .' Thus, fear is sneaking like a grey

29

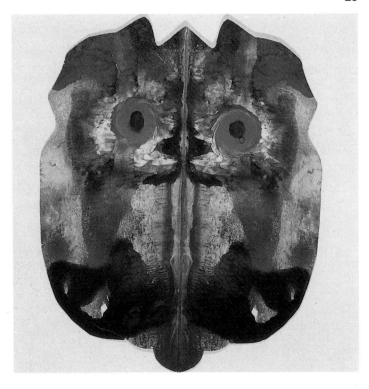

29 *Fear Makes One See Danger as Twice as Threatening.* The instructions for this work can be summed up as follows: 'Paint a mask of fear so that it vaguely reminds you of an owl. When you see it in the dark you get a terrific fright because at first you do not realise that it is just an ordinary owl.' The mask was created by holding the paper along its axis to transfer thicker tempera paints.

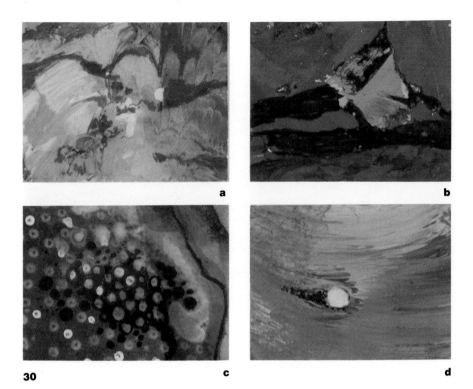

a

b

30

c

d

30 *Sunday Moods.* The children discovered these with the help of an oblong viewfinder made of white paper (8 x 6 cm). They moved it along an older cracked painting. When they came across an interesting colour surface, texture or shape, the children wrote down the mood or activity these small pictures reminded them of. They pencilled in the outlines of the most interesting pictures, often in contrasting moods. They then cut them out and made small changes using colours.

a) 'I look forward to free time on Sunday. I am going to do what I want. I might feel like running round a football pitch or a field.'

b) 'We are going on a trip to the mountains on Sunday. I cannot wait to get away.'

c) 'My worst fears came true. The weather forecast for Sunday is bad and on top of it I have got a sore throat. It looks like a rotten Sunday!'

d) 'On Sunday I am going to a fairground. I love riding on the merry-go-round. I feel like an astronaut or a pilot when going round and round.'

snake; sadness is like a grey rain; happiness glows like a candled birthday cake or is like a clown in a multicoloured costume or a parrot swinging on its perch. If children paint 'fear' only in colour and shape, they soon realise that to express it they have to paint rather more than, for example, a snake. A picture of sneaking fear only retains the snake's symbol and its poisonous colour.

31

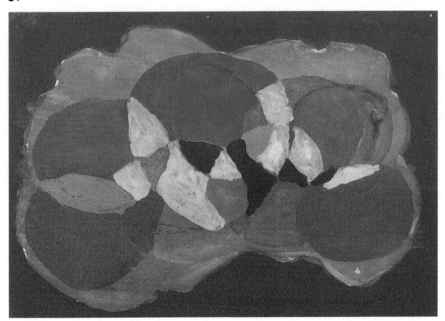

31 *A Ball Game.* A boy expressed in colour not only the happiness which accompanies the game but also the variety of ball movements. The same method can be used to find out how children might express activities such as skipping, riding a bicycle or ice skating through shape and colour.

30

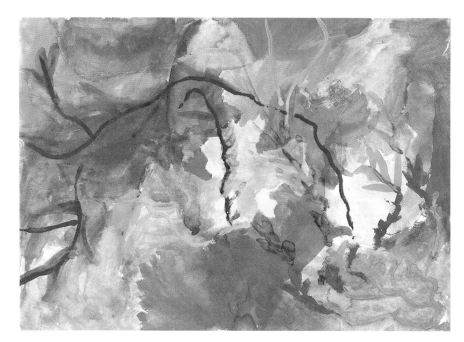

32 *Ballet on Tiptoes* is a coloured record of impressions from watching ballet dancers perform. Colours float tenderly; soft brushstrokes remind us of graceful hand and body movements.

33 *A Witch Flying on Her Broom.* This picture portrays movements which contrast in colour and shape with the movements of the ballet dancers in the previous picture. The streaming hair and the broom's bristles exaggerate the flying motion. They capture a sense of movement in the same way as lines are used, for example, in comics. Renaissance painters already knew how to convey the flickering movement of an object in paint.

In the pictures which the children refer to as 'happiness', they tried to capture movements in coloured lines and shapes. For example, the happiness experienced by a child when riding a bicycle, jumping over a skipping rope or dancing. The colours are arranged as if they were traces of a track along which an object moved in time, that is, as a record of the passage of time.

If children are able to paint movement can they paint taste?

33

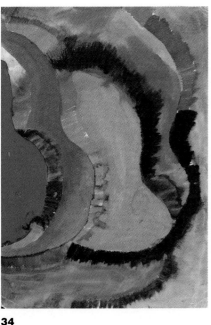

34

35

When children close their eyes for a second we can place a slice of lemon, a piece of chocolate, some pepper or a pinch of salt on their tongue. We can then ask them to paint the 'taste' in colour. If we want to tease them a little we can cut a slice of a huge watermelon for everybody but allow them to eat it only when they have painted how large and coloured the taste of melon is.

It has already been said that impressions of hearing are con-

36

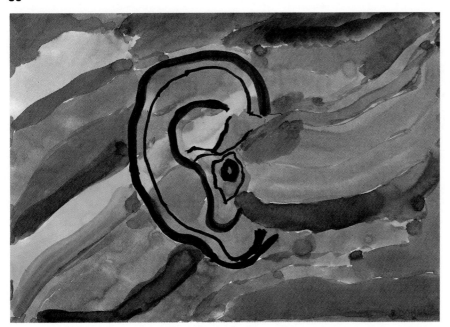

37 *Listening to Organ Music.* A younger girl who heard organ music for the first time attempted to demonstrate visually her impressions in tempera paint. For J.S. Bach's Toccata in E flat she selected wide strokes of a palette knife which corresponded to her impression of the music. Children can express the sounds of a harp, a trumpet or a violin in various ways.

nected with subjective notions of colour. For example, the Russian painter Wassily Kandinsky (1866—1944) perceived colour as 'a means of directly influencing the soul. Colour is a piano key. The eye is a sonic hammer.' Kandinsky was not the only one to think like this. Other painters also understood the hidden musical meaning of colour. Like melodic sounds and tones, colours themselves can appeal in combinations — tones — either pleasantly, as if effortlessly oscillating and floating, or unpleasantly, as if awkwardly falling into a deep ravine. The first visual images of music are in fact the rapid and excited or slow and soft movements of the conductor's hands when directing an orchestra.

We can attempt this interpretation of music with children while they listen to a musical composition. We ask them to tell us what their colour images are when they concentrate on listening. A flute may sound like rolling and tinkling rainbow marbles; the sound of a violin may remind them of green branches swinging in the wind.

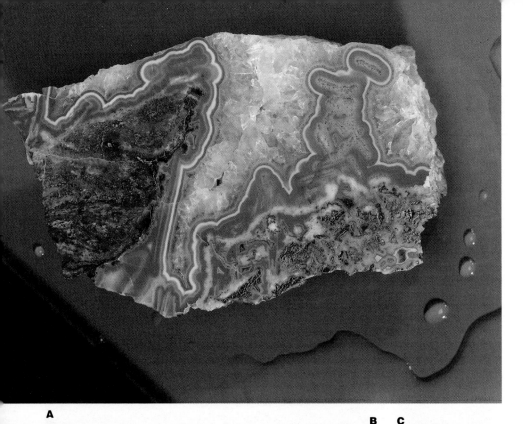

A *Polished Agate.* Are you also curious about how the colour red enters the stone's inside?

B *Bearded Cacti* are very interesting when they are blossoming. How do all those bright colours appear in their prickly bodies, in their rounded 'green structures' which remind us of a fantastic town?

C *A Barbed Wire House* surrounded by scaffolding looks like a huge cactus. How would its blossoms look?

D Aleš Lamr, *Teleskopka,* 1989, acrylic canvas (180 x 145 cm). This pleasing painting reminded the children of a curious animal or an instrument, also of a cactus or a strange building.

Illustrations on these two pages are similar. Can you discover similarities? (The pictures are connected through their 'mood', the colour green, their cactus shape, a resemblance to fantastic architecture and their 'curious' contact with the environment.)

A

B   **C**

3

39

38 *How Leaves Age from Spring to Autumn.* An older girl toned a wet sheet of paper downwards, starting with light 'spring' colours, which then changed into richer shades of green and finally turned from brown to fiery autumnal shades. When the colour washes dried she drew the outlines of leaves thinly and painted out the background with a thicker (second) layer of colour.

39 *The Sunshine in Spring, Summer, Autumn and Winter.* A child imagined the sun in the middle of the paper. The sunshine, which differs during each season of the year, affects Nature's colours also. Can you guess which quarter of the paper represents spring, summer, autumn and winter? The sunshine is painted from the centre outwards with diluted tempera paints.

Nature's Calendar on a Palette

Changes in Nature occurring from spring to winter. Portraits of the seasons. Colour coding of individual months. Calendars.

When we ask children which four colours they associate with the four seasons of the year, their answers may be quite similar. Light green for spring; red-orange for summer; brown for autumn and light grey for winter. However, since the children's answers may also differ, we can ask them to mix watercolours and create individual colour impressions of the twelve months of the year. When children explain their choice of colour, they often provide examples of characteristic colours in Nature (plants, trees, fields, woods) and typical weather (rain, fog, snow). They try to recall what Nature is like during a particular month.

40

40 *Sun-Changes Throughout the Four Seasons* were recorded by an eleven-year-old boy using felt-tip pens. He considered how green varies throughout the year and how much yellow, red, brown or blue appears in Nature according to each season. He worked on four small square sheets of paper simultaneously, and compared the amount he used of a specific colour on each square as he went. The spring sun is situated in the top left-hand corner.

However, if they go out 'hunting' for lighter and darker shades of an individual colour, they will realise that colours in Nature are not a simple matter. The simplest task might be to compare and arrange shades of green leaves. In the same way a whole shade sampler of red, blue and yellow colours can be created from a garden full of flowers. When children have arranged the shades of

41

41 *Colours in Nature from Spring to Autumn.* Tempera paints and a broad brush were used to paint this picture. The child painted on the whole area of the paper. First he dipped the brush in green and had to decide where to put most of the paint and where the least. He did the same with each of the other colours in turn.

42 *Spring Wakes up in a Well*. A younger child, painting from imagination, showed how in spring the ice thawed and clear water appeared inside a well. Using ink, the child then discovered a portrait of a creature, perhaps that of a sprite, who wakes up in spring.

one colour, and glued them onto a piece of paper, can they prepare the same colours by mixing tempera paints? Younger children can try to paint summer directly from Nature by using blueberry and raspberry juices or rubbing green leaves. It is fascinating how many colours can be discovered in Nature.

Fairy tales, legends and myths often reflect the four seasons of the year. The personification of Nature reflects the whole of human life from birth (spring) to death (winter). There is an old belief that if a well is cleaned after winter its first drops of clear water will have healing properties. Greek mythology populated springs and wells with mysterious female creatures. We might take

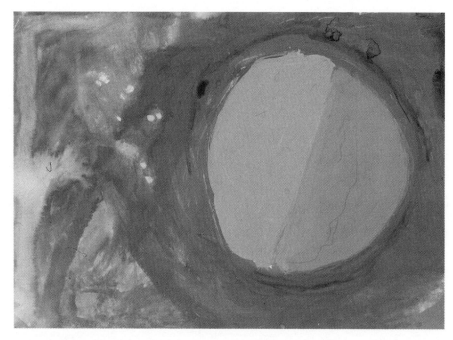

43

younger children for a walk in early spring to discover a well. We can tell the children a story of the well being enchanted and then being woken up after a harsh winter: 'Spring's Awakening'.

Children can later try to paint the well as a living creature. We

44

43 *A Well with 'the Water of Death*
This painting, in tempera paints, ex presses the idea of the Water of Death which is dangerous to all live creatures and organisms. In various shades o grey, the tempera paints are thick and suggest a motionless quality.

44 *A Well with 'the Water of Life*
This picture contrasts in colour with the previous one. The magical properties of healing waters are expressed in a more pleasantly coloured image. The colours are embedded into the we surface. The details of plants were added only when these areas had dried.

45 *Spring's Overcoat.* Children first drew and then cut out a small fairy tale character. They then selected pieces of coloured material which expressed the colours of spring and glued them onto the figure. After trimming the edges Spring's overcoat was ready.

46 *Summer's Wear.* This allegorical figure of the Summer Queen is wearing a long dress in colours which are typical of Nature in this season.

This Instructional Illustration shows a range of spring colours.

45   46

can also suggest that they try painting colour images of two fairy tale wells: one containing 'the water of life', and the second containing 'the water of death'. In this way they differentiate two colour images: one for the well in spring and one for the well in winter. It is important for children to realise that clean water is the provider of life on Earth; that it is linked to life's origin and to Nature's life cycle.

Many other creative opportunities are provided by the personification of Nature. Children are aware that they have different clothes for spring, summer, autumn and winter in their wardrobes. If they conceive of Nature as a creature, then it also should have a wardrobe of clothes. Children can produce collages or work with tempera paint, as shown in Pictures 45 and 46. They could imagine a Barbie doll which has a dress made of April showers and a dandelion hat for spring; and a rainbow swimming costume and a butterfly parasol for summer. To represent autumn, children could produce scarecrows and overcoats made from autumn leaves,

47

47 *Uncle Autumn Looking through the Leaves.* The child started this work by embedding typical colours of autumn onto a wet sheet of paper: the colours of fallen leaves, empty fields, drying hay or autumn fruit. A larger area in the centre of the paper was left for Autumn's face. Only a few details were needed to outline his face.

These Instructional Illustrations remind us of typical autumnal and winter colour tones. When painting the portraits of autumn or winter younger children can find inspiration in these.

and for winter they might make a snowman's overalls, icicle dressing gowns or snowflake hats.

Children can also do large portraits in colours which characterise a particular season or a month. Children can decide on the colours using their previous work (Pictures 38, 39, 40, 41). It should not be necessary to explain that Uncle Autumn's face or Auntie Winter's face will be in different colours from those of a human face but suggest that the children first plan the whole portrait in characteristic colours. Tell them to paint in layers and not to

48 *A Portrait of Auntie Winter.* This was painted in tempera. The artist assigned large areas for the face, hair, body and background. Since she was painting a portrait of winter she used a lot of brilliant white but toned it with blue and black. The girl alternated paste painting with washed-out areas where the colour was thinner and lighter. She added the eyes, nose and mouth and the snowflake decorations after the surfaces had dried.

48

bother too much about details. The title given to the painting, along with the painting itself, should make it clear whether children painted a Spring Bride or a Polar Blizzard; an Autumn Lady of Sorrows or a Summer Sunflower.

Older children can be further challenged to produce a calendar. Each of the twelve pages of the calendar should attempt to capture a particular colour tone matching its respective month complete with a simple characteristic detail. Divide the task amongst four children. The first one can decide on three colour images for

43

BŘEZEN · MAPT · MARCH · MARS · MÄRZ · MARZO

49

49 *First Spring Month — a Calendar List.* An older boy characterised this month using several rich colours, a shape and typical detail. He provided the following commentary for his picture: 'This month is a gateway to spring and sunshine, bringing life to everything. A plant begins to sprout in the brown, warm soil.'

spring, and so on. If spring as a whole is associated with green, it is up to the individual child to decide how to shade the colour green for these three months on colour surfaces and how much space to devote to it.

It is useful to talk to children while they are working and ask questions. For example, which shade of green are they going to use and how much space will be given to expressing a shy early month of spring? How will the colour green change in the showery middle month and which colours will be added to it in the third month when spring is at its height? How much yellow or brown is needed to balance the arrival of 'green spring'? In which month will white appear to remind us of blossom on the trees? Similarly, the second child will have to decide about colour for the summer months and the third child for the autumn months. Finally, the fourth child will try to differentiate in colour the more difficult months of winter.

The arrangement of coloured areas may remind children of fields, clouds, puddles, tree tops, piles of leaves or snowdrifts. At the end the children must decide on one objective detail which will identify a particular month precisely and which will also set the colour tone for the entire composition. Children should try to asso-

50 *Middle Spring Month — a Calendar List.* This picture can be explained as follows: 'This month is a changeable month when it suddenly starts to rain but a moment later the sun shines. Water in puddles provides replenishment for all the green plants. In the soil water rises to plant roots; it evaporates only to return as rain.' The picture itself was produced by embedding colours into a wet area.

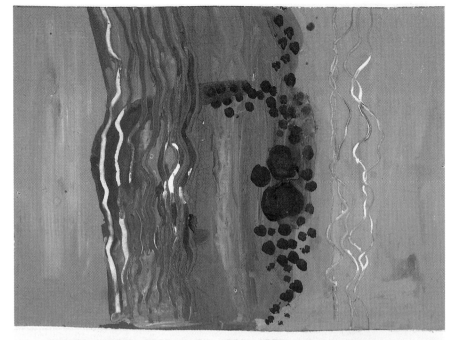

DUBEN · АПРЕЛЬ · APRIL · AVRIL · APRIL · ABRIL

50

51 *Signs of the Zodiac for August, September, October and November* were produced by an older boy in this alternative calendar. He coloured the signs using felt-tip pens. The individual subject motifs have a simplified shape and colour. They all appear in small rectangles. They are also examples of the decorative activities discussed in Chapter 9.

ciate a particular month correctly with its respective detail, such as a daffodil, a sailing boat, strawberries, a mushroom, yellow leaves, tree blossoms, ripe cherries, a football or a beach ball.

Creating calendars can also be understood as a whole year project. Every month children put various motifs and their colour studies into the cardboards and in December choose the most appropriate items for preparing the twelve sheets of the year.

51

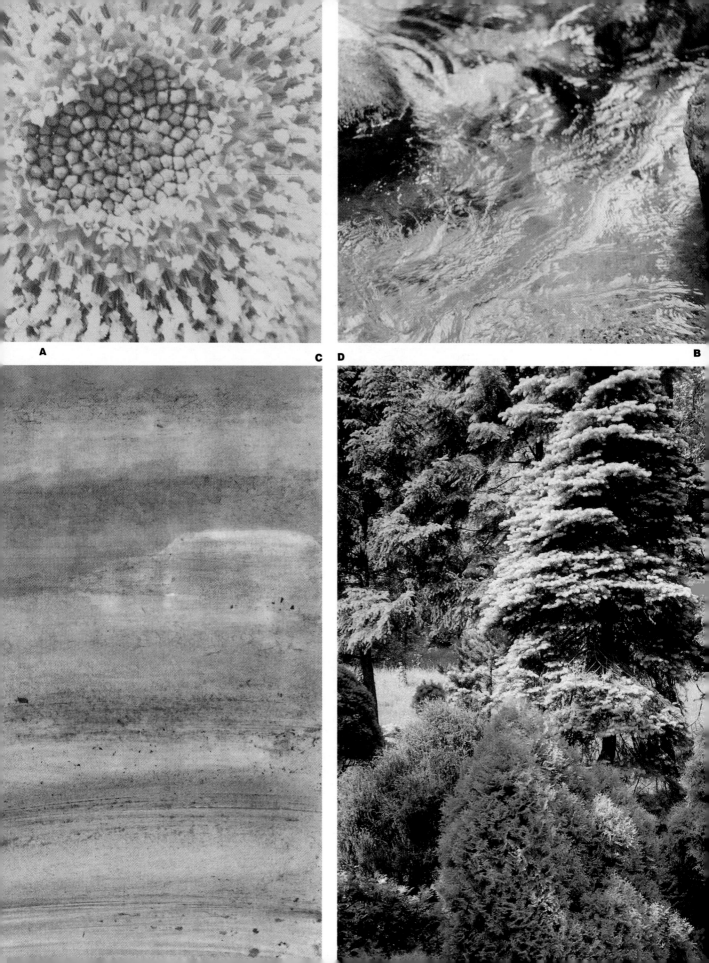

A

C D B

A *The Yellow Blossom* is composed from many warm rays like the sun itself.

B *Water in Spring* provides nourishment to all green plants.

C *Spring's Colours.* The colours on the sample were created by rubbing green grass and the flowers of dandelions, tulips and irises.

D *Counting Tones of Green* in spring is very interesting, especially if the trees and bushes bask in bright sunlight.

E

F

E Jiří Patera, *In Bud*, 1982, oil on canvas (60 x 75 cm). It seems as if a magic letter or an urgent signal is included in the sleeping Earth's memory. A little patch of green is symbolic of new life.

F Ivan Kafka, *A Very Bizarre Spring Hill,* 1988, green and red crepe 'grass' (height 550 cm, diameter 400 cm). Spring is like a huge 'time clock'. It is not only time that flows but weather, colours and feelings when winter ends.

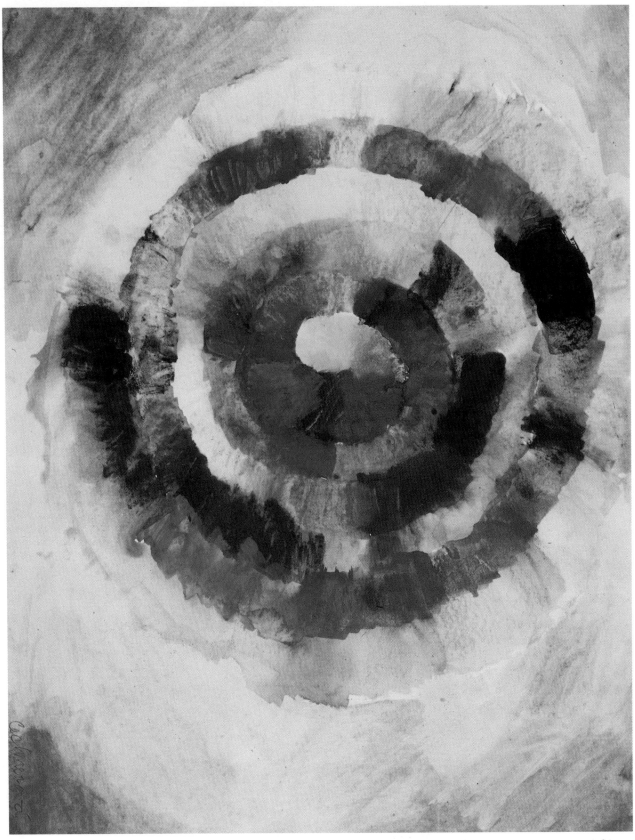

4

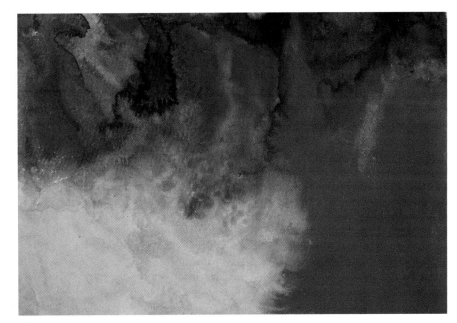

53

52 *The Sleeping Rainbow.* This painting was created after a story that the sun's rays were not able to squeeze through a wall of heavy rain. In order to make it easier for the sun's rays, the children broke the wall down into a rainbow, that is a fan of coloured lights of uneven wavelengths — starting with red, followed in turn by orange, yellow, green, blue and finally violet light. When the rainbow wakes up and spreads itself in a coloured bow its colours are arranged. Using a palette knife the children applied tempera paints directly from the tube in a spiral. They then washed the empty areas with water. Later they painted the risen rainbow with the colours in order of the spectrum.

53 *A Confluence of Three Coloured Rivers.* Red, yellow and blue rivers flow into a huge lake. In the wet area of the paper each pair of primary colours created its respective secondary colour. The children observed the creation of coloured tones: orange, green and violet. They then cut out white paper fish and tried to colour them so that they would appear invisible in a particular place on the lake.

Colours
and Their Regular Arrangement

Primary and secondary colours. Painting is the art of deciding colour schemes. What is the nature of colours?

Every colour only exists in relation to its closest surrounding colour. Colour does not exist in isolation. We might compare it with humans. They also do not live on their own. Each colour, like a human, has its family, its close and more distant relations. We might also say that colour has, like a human, its friends and enemies. It can quarrel or live peacefully. It can even shout out loudly if the colours surrounding it are quiet and calm. In a picture, colours as a whole can throw light on the real or imagined colour of objects; light and dark colours can model 'the roundness' of an apple; some colours are warm whereas others are cold. At other times colours can arrange themselves in such a sophisticated composition that the eye perceives them as rotating, undulating or sinking on a surface. Children have already learnt something

49

54   **55**

54 *Confusion on the Palette.* Rich pure colours were mixing — talking together — until they completely lost their original brightness.

55 *A Clown on Horseback Riding Through the Mud.* The painter tried to retain the very bright colours of the horse's blanket. The background is completed with less bright colours. Thus, the brightness seems to be shinier the 'muddier' the background is.

56 *Conversations Amongst Colours on the Palette.* Children imagined an arrangement of colours on a palette just before the painter starts his painting. The colours themselves are still glowing because they have not yet engaged in conversations.

about colour, however they will only comprehend and master colour relationships — contrasts and affinities — on the basis of more conscious activities.

Generally speaking, there are three primary colours — yellow, red and blue — in pigments. We can imagine these as three rivers flowing into a lake where their currents blend (as seen in Pic-

56

57 *The Green Dragon in its Fiery Lair.* This picture was painted with a pair of contrasting complementary colours, red against green, in order to make the monster 'bellow' loudly. Green is the furthest away from red in the six-coloured circle. It was created by mixing two primary colours — blue and yellow.

58 *The Yellow Dragon in a Violet Lair.* This picture also involves a pair of contrasting complementary colours. The violet colour is toned down by white, thus rendering the picture not so dramatic. In places even the yellow is 'muddied'. Another, third, picture could have been painted — that of the orange monster in a blue lair, using the third contrasting complementary pair in the six-coloured circle.

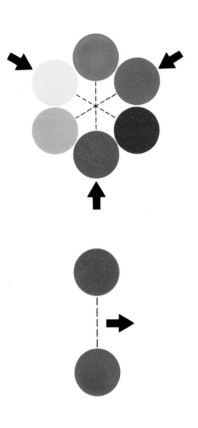

The six-coloured circle is composed of three primary colours with adjacent secondary colours. The opposite pairs of colours are in marked complementary contrast.

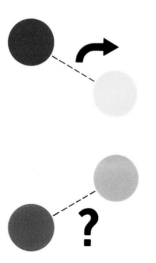

57

ture 53). In this activity we are going to use cadmium yellow, carmine and cobalt. Children can start by depicting on paper those areas where two primary colours blend and their related secondary colour is 'born'. The red and yellow colours blend into orange; the blue and yellow colours into green and the red and blue colours into violet. All three primary colours and their

58

51

59

60

59 *A Portrait in Three Primary Colours.* A boy placed tracing paper over a larger photograph. Using a felt-tip pen he marked the lightest areas of the face with lightest yellow and the darkest areas with darkest blue. For the semi-shadows he selected red as red is neutral from the light point of view.

60 *A Colour Negative of Picture 59.* In this picture a contrasting complementary violet replaces the light yellow colour and the darkest blue is replaced by the complementary lightest orange. Red, neutral from the light point of view, is replaced by a neutral complementary green. Pictures 59 and 60 were painted by the same boy. In his work he followed the Instructional Illustration below, which demonstrates the complementary contrast and the light contrast.

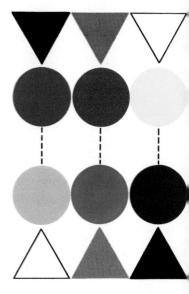

secondary colours, that is orange, green and violet, are rich and bright.

Children will later discover that if the three primary colours blend in the lake in even ratios, the resulting colour will be a dark grey-black colour. However, if the colours blend in uneven quantities then the resulting colours might be, for example, muddy 'olive' green colours, 'chestnut' browns or 'plum' blues, where the rich bright tone has disappeared.

The richness and brightness of all pure colours can be subdued by applying non-bright colours: grey, white and black. Younger children often make the mistake of preferring and considering correct only those colours which they feel to be rich and bright. If they 'muddy' colours they worry that they have made a mistake. It may be necessary to explain that all those less bright, unsaturated or cloudy shades provide an excellent background for the more expressive rich and bright tones which stand out in the picture. This is in fact a 'saturation' contrast. Children, however, understand it as a contrast between bright and less bright colours. Pictures 54 and 55 illustrate this point.

We can also discover another contrast — the 'complementary' contrast. In this activity six colours 'hold hands together' and create a circle (page 51). The arrangement of colours is not random — the three primary colours are adjacent to their respective secondary colour. Remember this arrangement well — orange shines between red and yellow colours; green is situated between

61 *Glass Binoculars.* The children put tempera paints on the bottom of several glasses. They rotated the glasses on the paper and observed through the bottoms the colours created. They attempted to differentiate primary and secondary colours; light and dark colours; bright and non-bright colours, and others.

61

yellow and blue; violet frowns between blue and red. Thus, the circle of six colours is complete. Which pairs of colours, across from each other in the circle, form contrasting complementary pairs? Red is furthest away across the circle from green; yellow from violet; blue from orange. They contrast as white day differs

62

62 *Recognising Colours in a Maze.* This work began as a game with several palette knives which are useful both for spreading tempera paints and for mixing them on paper. Using a viewfinder, the children looked for those colour arrangements which they could identify, such as the three primary colours or two contrasting complementary colours. They then cut their work into strips and were able to compose the lighter to darker colours of a particular colour tone.

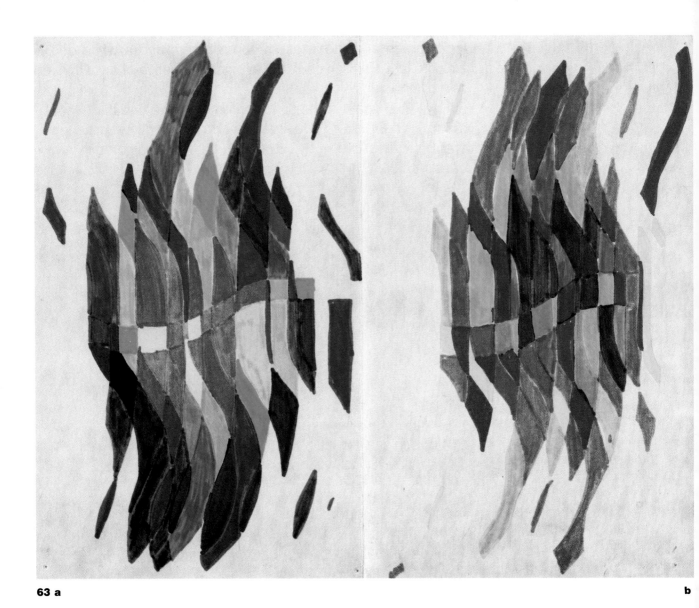

63 a   **b**

from black night. If two complementary pairs meet in a picture or in nature they call attention to themselves as if with a shout; red seems to be even redder next to green and vice versa. If we mixed them together they would become so 'muddied' that their original brightness would completely disappear.

Look directly at a bright red setting sun. If you then close your eyes you should experience under your eyelids a whirling disc in a contrasting green colour. Children can observe the world in contrasting colour reverse by comparing a colour photograph with its negative. When looking for complementary contrasting colours they will find that the yellow colours of a photograph appear in the negative as violet; the blue skies change to orange; a red cap

63 a) *Colours Caught in a Net.* The children first drew a net using a paper template (see Instructional Photograph). Then, using felt-tip pens, they selected colours starting with light warm ones in the middle squares and finishing with colder dark ones at the net's edges.

b) *Colours Caught in a Net* are in reverse order in this picture, with cool dark colours in the middle. These contrasts of colours create an optical illusion. The net seems to undulate.

54

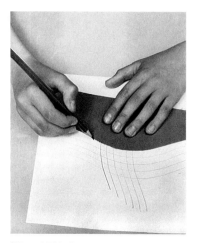

64 a) This involves a similar task to the variations of Picture 63. It is interesting to observe that the centre of the net composed of yellow, orange and red colours seems closer to the observer.

b) In this picture, the centre which is composed of cool dark colours seems to recede from the observer, as if it were falling into an abyss. All these nets are joyful coloured compositions whose solutions enable us to observe the contrast of light and dark colours, and the contrast of warm and cool colours.

looks green and green grass appears red; and a white dog is black. Older children could try to paint a negative of a yellow, red and blue face (Pictures 59, 60).

If we look again at the six-coloured circle we can discover another contrast: the 'light-dark' contrast. Yellow and orange are the lightest of the six colours. They are in light contrast with darker colours, the most conspicuous being violet and blue. We can lighten green and orange by using the lightest yellow. In combination with its complementary colour violet, yellow would only cause unfortunate muddying (remember the blending of the three primary colours). Of course, every colour can also be lightened by white or darkened by black. The entire 'family' of blue tones can be arranged from the lightest to the darkest shades of blue. The deep 'bluest' blue unblended with any other colour, that is without any traces of white or black, appears somewhere in the middle of the line. The initial lightest blue is in the greatest light contrast at one end and the darkest blue is at the other.

There is another method of creating contrast. Any colour can be lightened by diluting it with water. Children will recall what rain water achieved when it ran down dark temperas directly squeezed from the tube onto paper (Pictures 14, 15, 16). A heap of thick blue tempera became so diluted with water that the white

64 a

b

65

sheet of paper shone through the paint and the blue colour became lighter and lighter. This blue contrasted in both 'light' and 'saturation' with the blue tempera directly squeezed out of the tube. Children should learn how to use contrasting, differently structured areas. Note that watercolours are the most luminous colours.

In the previous chapter children discovered the 'warm-cold' contrast when they tried to paint a picture of winter (Picture 48) and imagined summer clothes (Picture 46). They divided the colours into 'warm' colours which contained mostly red and yellow and contrasting 'cool' colours which contained mostly blue. In this

65 *The Sun's Gate.* A girl distributed three diluted tempera paints — blue, yellow and red — on a surface. Using palette knives she then spread the paints and built a gate as if made from stone. The whole picture relies on the contrast between the bright and lighter background and the less brightly coloured dark gate. Large areas in the background are contrasted with smaller areas which employ subdued darker shades. The Sun enters and then leaves through the Sun's Gate.

66 a) *Sunrise Ushering in a Sunny Day.* Using layers of paints, an older child tried to position darker colder colours in the centre of a net of squares. These change into lighter warmer colours as they move out from the centre.

66   a   b

b) *Sunrise Ushering in a Cloudy Cold Day.* Darker colours are situated in the net's centre. They change into lighter cold and non-bright tones. It is only in black and white photographs of both paintings that we can observe what was impossible to see in the paintings.

contrast two opposite colours suggesting heat or cold are involved. It depends on the painter whether these colours will be light or dark, complementary or differently saturated. Children usually find this contrast between warm and cool colours interesting so the whole of the following chapter is devoted to this topic.

There are other contrasting relationships in the arrangement of colours. However, children may find it more interesting to learn about the nature of individual colours.

The colour yellow is the lightest colour. It shines joyfully and warmly as does the sun. But when it is even slightly muddied, then the sun suddenly becomes ill, wicked and treacherous. Yellow combined with red creates orange, while with blue it makes green. The more yellow is in green the lighter, livelier and warmer green becomes. The most contrasting colour with yellow is violet.

Children know the colour red in many guises. It may be either a darker carmine or a medium red. On its own red is not as light as yellow. However, it is as lively and joyful. It is the colour of blood; of ripe fruit; of fire and love. In comparison with other colours red seems to be full of energy. It is also a majestic, noble colour. In other instances we know it as the colour of prohibition, threat or even anger. Its most contrasting colour is green.

The colour blue is dark and cold and recedes into the distance of far-off lands or the depths of the ocean. That is why blue

67

reminds us of our longing for the mysterious; it can also evoke a sense of tranquillity, concentration and faith. If we add red to blue then various tones of violet appear. Different degrees of blue-greens, greens and light greens can be achieved by adding various quantities of yellow. Its most contrasting colour is orange.

The colour green belongs amongst darker and colder colours. However, as we mostly associate green with vegetation, its lighter yellow-green tones remind us of spring; of the birth of life in nature; of youth; of hope and promise. Green will not excite us as much as red, which is its most contrasting colour.

The colour orange is very warm. After all, it arises from yellow and red. It evokes notions of gold, wealth and maturity. It brings about a feeling of joy. In its brownish tone orange appeals like fresh fragrant soil. Its most contrasting colour is blue.

The colour violet is the darkest of all the colours. Children often associate it with fear. Violet is said to frown as if a thunder-

67 *Contrasts I.* In this picture children can review the types of contrasts they already know:

- the contrast of bright and less bright colours
- the complementary contrast of the most distant colours, such as red and green
- the contrast of dark and light colours
- the contrast of paste saturated surfaces and surfaces washed with water; paste surfaces are painted with a palette knife
- the contrast of large warm areas of red and smaller cold areas of green colour. In addition, this also employs the contrast of rival shapes — those of a circle and a square.

68 *Contrasts II.* The most striking contrast of all is the contrast of light shapes against a dark background. Both the circle and the square are comprehended here from the stand-point of the contrast between warmer and colder shades.

storm were about to occur. It is frightening. It could harm or even cast a spell over a person. However, when it is toned with white, violet suddenly becomes warm and tender. Its most contrasting colour is yellow.

The colours black, grey and white are not always con-sidered to be colours by children, especially when they associate them with black and white television or a black and white photo-graph. However, black and white can significantly influence the colour mood if they are blended with bright colours, by making them either lighter or darker. If black and white are mixed in differ-ent ratios we get a scale of light to dark non-bright greys. By ad-ding blue, the tones of the colder greys arise. Adding small quan-tities of red results in a range of warmer greys. Black and white provide the greatest contrast of light. Together with grey they cre-ate an excellent background for other bright colours — they recon-cile them or make them stand out.

A

B

A *Coloured Water in Bottles.* The children prepared a sample of primary and secondary colours by inserting narrow bottles containing three primary colours into wider five-litre bottles also containing three primary colours. The secondary colours (violet, green and orange) appeared as a result of translucence.

Narrow two-coloured bottles are another 'discovery'. The children gradually inserted plastic bags in them and then poured in water coloured with ink. The bottles can be arranged and re-arranged according to their lighter and darker tones.

B *A Palette.* Looking at the arrangement of colours on a palette we can guess that the painter must have been painting a very bright bunch of flowers.

C Aleš Lamr, *Bella Vista,* 1989, acrylic canvas (180 x 145 cm). This merry-go-round created out of the primary and secondary colours celebrates our colour vision. The children can discover and name the contrasts — i.e., complementary contrast, contrasts of light and warmth.

C

70

69 *The Sun's Reflection in a Pond* was initially painted with diluted tempera paints on glass. The children then placed a sheet of paper on the wet glass surface. This resulted in an interesting print — a monotype which the children completed by painting their own impression of a warm sun reflected on the cold rippled surface of a pond.

70 *The Red and Blue Birds:* a red bird and a kingfisher. This tempera painting is based on a 'warm-cold' contrast. It was inspired by a story about two migrating birds which were similar in shape but which would rarely, if ever, meet. The red bird would arrive in the hot summer, while the blue bird would arrive and spend winter in a cold garden. The child painted these birds at the time when they exchanged places.

The Cold and Warm Palette

The Sun and Fire in warm colours. The cold world under the water and also above the clouds. Portraits of water sprites and mythical birds. Can Fire make friends with Water?

Even younger children find it easy to divide the coloured circle into emotionally warm and cool colours. They are keen to produce paintings motivated by pre-determined warm or cold colouring. We can further develop the feeling of the 'warm-cold' contrast in older children by working with cool and warm colours simultaneously. The ability to use the slightest warmth differences depends on sophisticated visual and technical skills. The children have to be able to prepare and also use subtly contrasting colour tones.

71

71 *The Hearth Goblin.* First, a younger child printed on his paper a fiery spot from diluted temperas mixed on glass. Onto this background the child painted, with a thinner brush, a household inhabited by a creature who keeps the hearth burning. People say that such little 'hearth goblins' existed in the past.

Before younger children start to paint, try to clarify their feelings about warm and cold colours in Nature and in the objective world around them. As an example of warm colouring we can mention a yellow summer sun; a red fire; a bright red kitchen stove; the blossoming of red poppies; the hot red cheeks of a feverish child. After

72

72 *How Logs Smoulder and Burn in the Hearth.* The children tested and tried possible shades of red. It is said that there are up to two hundred shades in a single red tone.

73 *The Water Goblin.* This picture is a contrasting cold variation of Picture 71. In this instance the cold background was also created as a monotype — a single print from a picture painted on a glass plate. The household of the goblin who looks after clean water is, however, furnished with different articles. It resembles a small laboratory or workshop.

these introductory talks children can start painting in tempera, for example, a mythical bird sitting on a golden apple tree; a hut where a fire goblin lives; a glowing sun or burning logs in the fireplace. They will only use bright warm colours, yellow, orange and red. In the next phase of painting the children can attempt shades of these

74 *Flood.* The shades of cool colours are arranged in a composition typical of water. They rotate, spin and whirl.

74

75

colours. They will soon discover that in order to retain the warmth of the derived shade (light yellow-green, red-violet, warm grey) they will have to add only tiny amounts of cold colour.

Cold colours can be used to paint a whole range of topics. For example: blue birds; a winter window blossoming with frost; an icicle maze — an ice cave; a portrait of the Snow Queen; portraits of fairy characters who live under the water (the Sea King) or in the blue skies (the North Wind). The illustrations offer further possible topics and the captions explain how the children proceeded in their work.

75 *The Fire Goblin.* A child painted his own impression of a mythological or fairy tale character. He used large colour areas which were later completed with the features of a face. Possible shades of warm colours are painted next to the picture itself. The colours were sprayed through a template onto a red background.

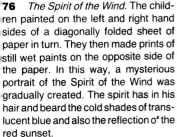

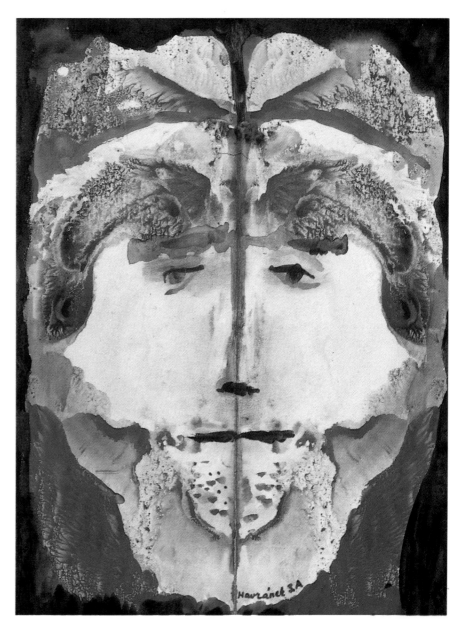

76

76 *The Spirit of the Wind.* The children painted on the left and right hand sides of a diagonally folded sheet of paper in turn. They then made prints of still wet paints on the opposite side of the paper. In this way, a mysterious portrait of the Spirit of the Wind was gradually created. The spirit has in his hair and beard the cold shades of translucent blue and also the reflection of the red sunset.

The picture is accompanied by an example of blue colours graded from light to dark.

At this time it might be appropriate to point out that children should make use of several brushes simultaneously: brushes for pure colours and brushes for dark and light shades. They should also be encouraged to test small amounts of tempera paint first on a clean spot on the palette or on a sheet of paper. Note that an appropriate amount of white will help to avoid paintings looking either too muddy or too bright. Encourage children to use the technique of embedding colours in a wet base. Children could be warned against frequently using undiluted paste colour squeezed directly from the tube onto the paper.

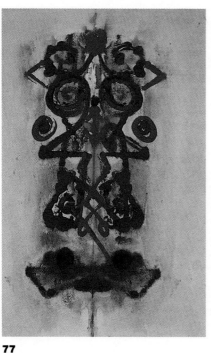

77

78

77 *A Household Totem.* This painting with a brush was executed in the same manner as Picture 76. It was inspired by a talk about tribal customs. In the past people believed there were gods who protected them from the hostility of the elements.

78 *A Confluence of Three Rivers.* This tempera painting is a triple portrait; a personification of a river with two smaller tributaries. The children used thinner brushes to complete the large areas in cool colours.

Many games are possible in relation to the arrangement and selection of colours. For example, ask children to put on all the 'green and blue' articles they can find in their wardrobe at home. They can then place stuffed stockings on their head; wear a blue T-shirt accompanied by a scarf or a towel; or use a bedspread in cold tones

79

80

79 *The Moonlight Reflected on a Pond's Surface* is a portrait of a water sprite. This bold tempera painting contrasts a warm yellow colour with its cold background. The moonlight reflected in the water may even suggest a creature watching us from the depths of the water.

80 *A Portrait of a Water Sprite* who guards thermal springs. The children first drew the water sprite's head in pencil. With a brush they then painted lines showing the flow of the water. It was then necessary to complete the face between the water lines. This made it possible to contrast the water sprite's cool colours with the warm colours of the thermal springs.

81 *A Water Sprite's Nature.*
In fairy tales the water sprite is
depicted as an ugly, grumpy
and wicked fellow. If he is old
he lives in swamps and bogs
as seen in our picture. The
base colour areas were executed on a wet surface with a
palette knife. The tempera
paints were then spread directly onto the paper and the
background given a wash
using a broad brush. This picture is an example of 'warmth'
and 'light' contrasts.

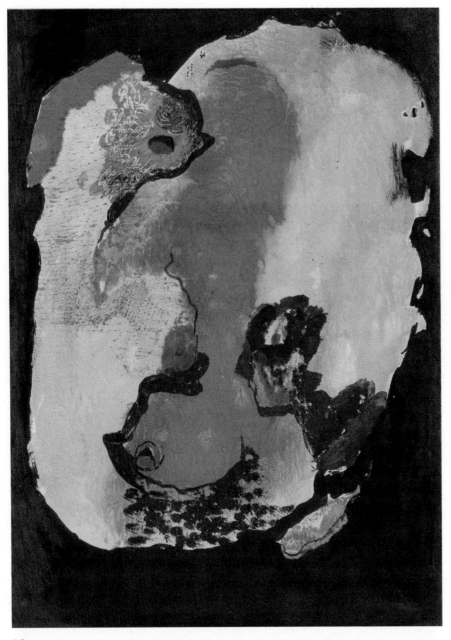

82

82 *The Sleeping Spark.* In prehistoric times people would light a fire by striking two flint stones together. A spark was created and fire began to burn. In this picture, the whole area of which was printed as a monotype, the spark is still slumbering. It looks as if a small red light is smouldering in a cold background.

as an overcoat. When children observe themselves in a mirror they might come up with the idea of painting a water sprite. In order to create a fantastic creature living in the clouds they could arrange an eiderdown and a pillow in suitable blue coverings on a sofa in front of a mirror, and then sit down in 'the blue skies' and observe themselves. Later they can paint a mysterious creature from memory.

In Pictures 69, 70, 82, 84 and 85, younger and even older child-

83 *The Awakened Fire.* This work is a monotype. The children painted an area of 'a fiery stone' with thick temperas on a glass plate. They then pressed a sheet of paper onto the glass and pulled it slightly, thus creating the flickering of a figure in the paste structure of the tempera. In painting the two variations of Sleeping and Awakened Fire (Pictures 82, 83), the children appreciated more fully the degree of tension caused by the application of smaller and larger quantities of vibrant red colour.

ren were asked to employ warm and cool colours in the one painting. The cool colours are contrasted with the warm colours by their clear bright nature and also by the reflected form of light and dark shades. Children can also be provided with more realistic experiences of observed colour changes. In a butterfly collection children can find one specimen with strikingly blue wings and a second with fiery red wings. It might be worth trying to paint the two butterflies with one wing exchanged for another. Or else we could ask the

84

children to pick two bunches of flowers. One bunch will consist of flowers in warm colours and the second of light and dark flowers in cool colours. The warm bunch can be placed in a jug against a cold background; the other bunch against a contrasting warm background. Or both bunches could be combined and then painted.

On their walks children can observe Nature through colour cellophane filters; in this way trees, clouds or even a pond change their colour. Combining several filters will create unusual colours. Children can magically create a sunset in the early afternoon using red, yellow and blue filters; the countryside just before a storm occurs; or a forest fire. The children can then paint these experiences of the countryside from memory.

Similar colour tricks can be prepared at home, for example, by changing the colour shade of a table lamp. A colour change can

84 *Sun and Water Hidden in a Stone.* This picture was painted after talking about the miracle which occurs each spring when plants sprout from seeds, pips and fruit stones. Every seed contains all the strength gathered in the previous year as it ripened. The sun and water hidden in a stone symbolise the two sources of life of the future

plant. This picture of an enlarged fruit stone was painted with diluted watercolours. The warm colour of the sun is contrasted with the cold colour of water.

85 *A Table Lamp Provides Pleasant Light and Warmth.* This emotional painting with diluted tempera paints was intended as a recollection of pleasant moments spent at home reading a book. The red lampshade delineates the warmly lit area under the lamp which is surrounded by its cold shadow.

85

Left: It is helpful to have examples of variously shaped stones, pips and seeds in order to provide real inspiration.

also be noticed by affixing a piece of red cellophane onto the lamp or simply placing a red scarf over it. Children will then be better able to capture the intimate warm atmosphere of a table in the evening, when the rest of the room is in colder semi-shade. They can do this even when painting from memory.

A trip to the many coloured locale of the zoo may also be very alluring for children carrying just a sketchbook and crayons.

A **B**

A, B *Thunderstorm Clouds.* Using a red filter a photographer — a meteorologist — changed these clouds into a frightening fire. Have you ever tried to 'change' Nature by viewing it through coloured cellophane filters?

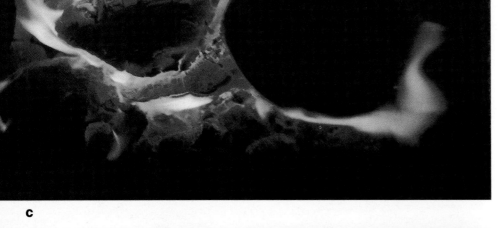

C *Fire.* People have always been attracted by a real fire — by burning logs in a fireplace. We experience pleasant heat, security and tranquillity.

C

D *Rapids.* We are affected differently by water, by its rippling, its vitality and its coolness. The colouring of water has many aspects. This painting evokes a feeling of freshness, or even of unrest.

D

E

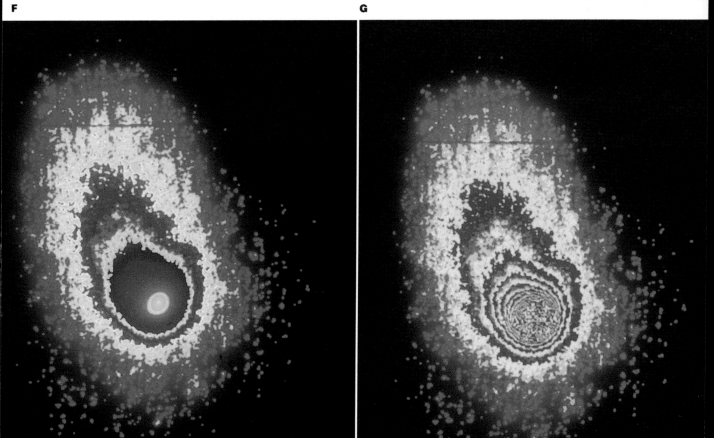

E, F, G *Halley's Comet* was photographed on 20 January, 1986, by Martin Setvák. He used a reflecting telescope at Prague's Petřín Observatory. This picture was processed several times by computer and different values were given to the so-called pseudo-colours. Thus, astronomers obtained valuable detailed data on the concentrations of dust and gases close to the Comet itself. Children may also find the Comet's changes of warm and cool colours of interest.

F

G

6

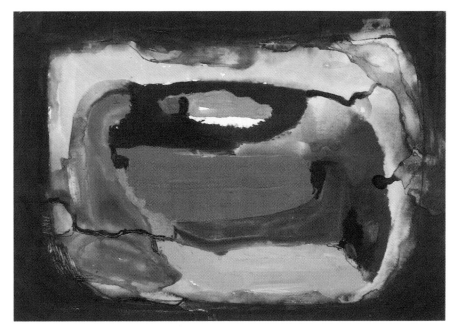

87

86 *Hunting for a Song Bird.* This painting in thick tempera was inspired by a talk about Robinson Crusoe wanting to catch a red song bird in the jungle. It was necessary to create a contrasting background in the multi-coloured jungle vegetation, as suggested by coloured spots, in order that the song bird might not be lost. This is the reason why the colours close to the bird are less bright, less dark and of a contrasting green.

87 *Red Skies.* This painting conveys a subjective feeling relating to the preceding night. The painter first painted dark clouds in thick temperas and later diluted them with water. Finally, he found a suitable spot for the accenting red colour.

Tension or Tranquillity in the Picture

How do we create a background for the colour red? Intensifying or suppressing colours. A coloured accent is a ray of light in the dark forest. The happy and sad countryside.

Through the natural colouring in children's paintings we can sense how much spontaneous pleasure or serene tranquillity is conveyed. In order to ensure that these are more than random occurrences, try to inspire children with those topics which will enable them to comprehend the relationship between a certain colour background and a definite colour. In this context we will only deal with the colour red as this seems to be the most attractive one to children. Also, red often becomes a colour accent.

The stressing of one colour — the colour accent — becomes an important element in arranging the colouring of a whole painting. For example, when painting a dark forest a light will suddenly ap-

88

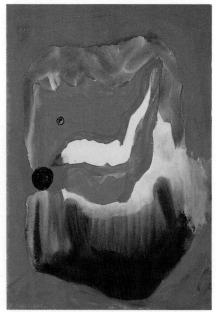

89

88 *Alone in the Rain Forest*. This painting in thick temperas on the whole surface of the paper captures a man's fear of unknown surroundings in which he feels defenceless and lost. Bright colours seem to attack him from all sides. The red helps to create tension; it is equal to the other bright colours.

89 *A Sudden Flash of Lightning*. This painting also involves the creation of a colour background in which to use red. It is inspired by a natural phenomenon. A tiny red accent seems to be a full stop to the sudden thunder and flash of lightning which lasted only for a fraction of a second and then faded away in our consciousness. Red finalises a greater accent of yellow.

pear — in a rich red colour — in the distance. It brings hope; sets us free from the dangers of dark colours; and catches the observer's eye. Some examples of colour accent are the final rays of the sunset; a red song bird in the forest; a climber's red tent at the foot of a threatening grey mountain range; a red sail on the horizon of a dark stormy sea.

90

91

90 *A Hill Changing Throughout the Day* was painted with tempera paints in three variations. As the amount of light diminishes we can imagine even more variations according to decreasing colour and light.

91 *The Sunset* in three variations. The glow of red and yellow gradually decreases.

92 *Getting Dark* was painted in three stages by an older boy. It represents the disappearance of red sky in the evening. Colour properties recede; contrasts of light and warmth fade away in the darker colours of the night; what is left of the day shines for a second in white and red as the final accent.

Below: Try to determine against which background red glows at its fiercest. Against which is it lighter? Against which is it darker? Against which background does it nearly disappear? What phenomena in Nature or the objective world do the individual squares remind you of? (A ball lying in the grass, and so on.)

92

Red colouring can either be intensified or suppressed. Children will soon understand the conscious use of accent if they paint a sunset or sunrise in several consecutive stages. At sunset the red skies gradually fade; in the final stage only a tiny red spot remains. This red spot will, however, shine twice as brightly in the darkness of the ensuing night.

93

Children can also investigate how the bright red changes its 'glare' against different backgrounds. They cut several big identical circles out of paper and then look for a single coloured background in the room. They place the circles, for example, on a green carpet, a white wall or a blue towel. They will soon discover that a light red is more expressive against a cold green background but loses its brightness against a warmly toned background. Older children can paint the changes of red against the background of a differently coloured landscape, such as a blue-green countryside with the red roof of a farmhouse; or a brown and grey autumnal landscape, including an isolated tree with fiery red leaves. In Pictures 93 and 94 the children used red in an unusual way. In both cases they painted a landscape dominated by the red surface of a pond. In the first painting the red pond conveys a sense of happiness and the landscape composed of fields, trees and hills reinforces this pleasant

93 *A Happy Pond Surrounded by the Fields* is a painting done in diluted temperas. The red water surface, painted at the beginning, is associated with a happy mood which is then reflected in the 'friendly' bright colours of the countryside. The pond is 'the eye of the countryside' and all the roads, fields and even trees are in a hurry to meet it.

94 *A Lake Surrounded by Mountains.* This painting bears on its reverse the following commentary: 'Oh, rock, why are you silent? Your heart turned into stone. Anyone who climbs you will forget everything that was ever dear to his heart.' The darker violet red of the lake's surface is a warning; a sign of danger. The colour accent of a tiny house where one can find a safe haven in this dark gloomy countryside might be the only hope. As in the previous painting, the children first painted the central red surface. However, they gave different meaning to the colour red in the way that they completed the colouring of the surrounding countryside.

atmosphere which becomes warm and bright. In the second painting the red surface of the pond is surrounded by dark trees, grey banks and black rocks. The red suddenly seems to convey a warning. More sensitive children may identify themselves with the colour surface of the lake which views the countryside as if it were the human eye. In this way they can observe how the black background entraps red and changes its significance.

Children can also consider colour changes in the countryside by looking at appropriate reproductions of paintings in magazines which they can colour in with felt-tip pens. Travel brochures and calendars often have good quality pictures of castles and chateaux which may be interesting for younger children. Children know from fairy tales that castles may be 'enchanted' and that wizards may live in them. Just imagine what sort of colour change will occur when the spell is broken and people are joyful because a huge wed-

95

96

ding is to be held! The people will decorate not only the castle but the town too. How else do people express their happiness, if not by colour?

With more pictures children can try out other variations. They could complete the castle with towers cut out from other pictures or cut out the castle itself and glue it in the midst of a desert or an ocean; on top of a steep rock or suspended in the blue skies. After all, fairy tales often tell of mysterious appearances and disappearances; castles being moved in time and space. When a collage is ready, children can unify the castle and its surroundings with felt-tip pens or inks as they wish. Felt-tip pens and inks are quite suitable for this because the picture itself will still remain visible under their colouring.

Older children can try to paint tension or tranquillity in a picture in two variations of the autumnal landscape. They know autumn as a

95 *The Sleeping Beauty and Her Castle.* The children coloured in a reproduction of a castle with felt-tip pens. The colours were selected in such a way as to convey a sense of mystery and threat. The colour pink seems to be enchanted, as if asleep amongst the darker colours.

96 *A Wizard's Castle.* A boy glued other towers to a magazine picture of a castle. He then unified the whole picture by colouring it in with felt-tip pens and inks. Lighter tones seem to flicker through the darker colours, as if the castle's lights were being switched on and off. The details in black emphasise the mysterious nature of the castle.

97 *A Happy Wedding.* A younger child completed a picture of a Renaissance summer villa with coloured felt-tip pens. In the past, great celebrations would have been held there with fireworks. These bright decorations are in contrast with the enchanted castles above.

98 *A Happy Castle.* This painting also involves an occasion of rejoicing. A 'liberated' town is decorated with coloured bunting, as mentioned in fairy tales. A magazine picture was coloured in with felt-tip pens.

97

98

99

99 *The Melancholic Autumn Land-scape.* An older boy painted this with diluted covering paints. The painting evokes a mood of tranquillity and quiet sadness in late autumn. The boy first pencilled in the fundamental divisions of the whole slope with several simplified shapes of houses. He then made the areas wet so that the colours would dissolve evenly. Finally, he painted the trees with a thinner brush. The non-bright colours contrast slightly with one another according to light and warmth.

fireworks display of warm bright colours but it can also be foggy with fading colours and evoke a melancholic mood. Children may find inspiration during a walk in the park or in the country, or they could merely imagine the countryside.

As they paint these two variations children will realise which colours evoke a sense of tranquillity and sadness and which evoke a sense of tension, excitement or even apparent movement. Pictures 101 and 102 illustrate that even a still life with fruit can be painted differently in accordance with the child's ideas.

100 *Sunshine in an Autumn Landscape*. The colour mood of this painting contrasts with Picture 99. Yellow shines brightly amongst other warm colours. It seems to run wild on most of the surface. Small colour surfaces bounce off each other. They are painted with paste colours which were later given a wash. The painting itself is clearly not tranquil, neither in its structure nor in its use of contrasting warmth and light. It was painted with the intention of portraying the tension in an autumn landscape.

100

The individual approach in painting the countryside or a still life will help children to understand that any reality, or its objective photography, shows every observer the same general and impersonal features but may be rendered in various ways. The author's expression reveals the truthfulness of painting.

101 *Still Life with Fruit*. This painting is lively; tension is created by the colours, shapes and lines. The colours are pure and bright. A marked contrast of black and white is noticeable. The tension is also stressed by a black line which winds its way throughout the whole still life.

102 This painting is a serene variation of Picture 101. The colours are subdued by white, the contrasts of warmth and light are slight so that the painting looks faded. There is no pure bright colour; a line does not undulate here. These still lifes were not painted from a model.

101

102

A *Polished Jasper from Kozákov Hill.* The stone's contrasting colours seem to be revealing the huge drama which took place during its creation. The picture reminded the children of the head of a green dragon engulfed in flames.

B Jaromír Rybák, *The Sacrifice Stone,* 1988, cut and painted glass sculpture (28 x 36 x 42 cm). The shape and colour of this sculpture reveal the secret of reconciling the anger of Gods through ritual sacrifice. The colours are of symbolic significance.

A

B

C Jiří Patera, *Prospero's Island I,* 1982, oil (80 x 65 cm). This painting evokes feelings of both tension and conciliation. It seems as if the noble colour red is the colour of the wise ruler Prospero who was in exile on an island in distant seas. He can magically unleash elements. Prospero is also a character in *The Tempest* by William Shakespeare.

D, E *The Red Leaves* of a thermophilic plant seem to be brighter and 'redder' on the contrasting rich green background.

D

E

C

103

7

104

104 *A Magnified Cluster of Quartz Crystals* painted with diluted tempera paints. Pink crystals had to be painted in darker shades to show their symmetrically arranged plane faces, some reflecting more light than others. These pink crystals were positioned against a very dark background in order to make them easier to observe. The background was painted last.

103 *Still Life with Three Jugs.* This picture was painted by a younger girl who used tempera paints over the whole area in the local colours selected by the potter. Likewise, the colour of the oranges and lemons was bestowed by Nature.

104 *A Magnified Cluster of Quartz Crystals* painted with diluted tempera paints. Pink crystals had to be painted in darker shades to show their symmetrically arranged plane faces, some reflecting more light than others. These pink crystals were positioned against a very dark background in order to make them easier to observe. The background was painted last.

Colours, Objects and Our Eyes

What is the colour of a jug or of an orange? Determining the colour of textiles. How to paint round balls. Colour contrasts when painting still life.

When dyeing a jug or a piece of material both the potter and the dyer mix one colour only. By doing this they determine whether the jug will be brown or the cloth green. When we speak about a red tomato or a golden-coloured orange we have in mind a specific colour. The colour orange of an orange is its local, i.e. real, colour. Children can quite easily determine the local colours of objects and mix them from tempera paints. If they place a sample of the colour orange against the skin of a real orange they can easily see whether they have managed to capture the identical local tone.

105

106 b

Using only local tones they could then paint several objects grouped in a still life as shown in Picture 103.

It is interesting for children to experiment with trying to extend in paint on paper a coloured piece of material in easily recognisable local colours. Children glue the material onto a sheet of paper and try to capture its colours and pattern in tempera. If the colours are properly observed and the tempera paints well mixed the material should appear to continue onto the paper. This activity becomes

107

105 *A Clown's Hat.* The children glued a piece of material onto a sheet of paper and tried to paint similar colours and shapes with tempera paints around the material. They mixed paints on smaller pieces of paper which they checked against the material or painted directly onto the paper. They painted the clown's face and the background using the surplus paint on their brushes, thus giving the painting a uniform colour tone.

106 a) *A Green Hat.* The piece of material glued in the middle of the paper has an abstract design so it was relatively easy to continue painting around the material in patches and small dots.

b) *A Blue Hat* is based on a piece of material which has a more complicated floral design — petals had to be arranged close to the material and close together on the paper in order to make the link with the material lifelike.

The same child painted all three hats. He then placed the cut-out hats on the clown's head. It was interesting to observe how the face changed depending on the hat's colour.

107 *Coloured Rags.* Crumpled pieces of material were laid on a grey base on a table. The children first pencilled in the basic outlines of the rags on a grey sheet of paper. They then used tempera paints to paint the brightest material, red and blue, in local colours. When these colours had dried, they became the determining factors for the lighter and darker shades of red and blue in the creases. The white piece of material on the grey base 'glows' and even its shadows are lighter than the grey base. The linear decoration was added at the end.

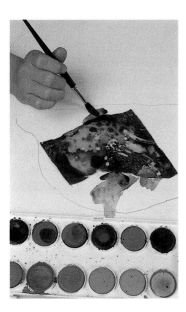

108 *My Mother's Best Sunday Hat.*
This tempera painting based on a piece
of material glued onto paper is an
example of how younger children can
use the colours and design of a piece of
material as an inspiration for their own
painting. The hat resembles a front garden, a landscape or a bunch of flowers.
This painting does not involve much
shape completion of the material design — the children were more interested in the colours they observed on
the material.

108

simpler if the material has an interesting abstract design which can
be developed, as seen in Pictures 105 and 108.

However, if we crumple single-coloured pieces of material and
place them on a table they become wavy; light and shadows appear in creases and the local colour changes slightly. To make the
point, crumple a white sheet in front of children. They know that the
fully stretched sheet is pure white but now that it is crumpled it is no

109

109 *Anoraks and Overcoats Hanging on a Peg.* An older boy selected this topic. He divided the warm and cold contrasts by painting a grey overcoat in the middle. For the wallpaper background he selected a grey and green colour, which is neutral from the warmth point of view. First, he drew simplified vertical blocks in pencil, on which he marked pure local colours — blue, pink, red and grey in tempera paints. He also marked those places which he observed as the darkest and compared them with the lightest places. He painted the background with diluted tempera paints. The small detail of a white appliqué is not a random decorative element. It helps to determine precisely the lightest place in the cluster of clothes.

longer simply white. The procedure for painting undulating pieces of material is explained in the commentary to Picture 107.

Older children may enjoy the challenge of trying to paint a two-tone colour maze, for example, a huge knot created by tying together two strips of red and green material. Hang the knot on a white wall or fix it on the door of a dark wardrobe. Coats and anoraks hanging on a peg or simply thrown over a chair might be other suitable models. When selecting a model first consider their light and

110 *Still Life*. In painting this still life composed of a piece of red and green material, a brown guitar and a jug, the intention was to compare the two most contrasting colours, red and green. First, the children pencilled in the fundamental contours. Then they painted the brightest pure colours — red and green — in tempera. Finally, they compared dark areas adjacent to lighter areas. The guitar's shape remained visible because its light green is contrasted with the dark green of the background.

111 *Still Life*. This painting was created as a rapid record of shapes. However, the colour contrast of red and green and the light contrast were preserved. This still life is lively despite the fact that it has not been completed. In this case the line contributes to the differentiation of the shapes.

110   **111**

colour contrasts. Small bright patterns or stripes may make a lively accent in the picture. Children should paint draped clothes in simplified local colours on smaller and larger surfaces and also in the areas of lighter and darker tones as caused by the light falling on crumpled material. Painting in tempera with a broad brush makes this simplified blocking of colour ratios on huge surfaces easier. It

112

112 *Apples and a Piece of Crumpled Paper*. Thick tempera paints spread with the incisive strokes of a broad brush created the light, shadows and different structures of an irregular and a round object. This topic was selected to enable the children to observe a significant warmth contrast — warm yellows and reds against a cold blue-green background.

113

does not involve reproducing the coats exactly but, rather, deciding which contrasts and colour qualities the children should observe. In fact, this entails a constant comparing of colours: bright — non-bright; cold — warm; light — dark. A single colour cannot be determined by itself, wherever it is. It is brighter or lighter, softer or darker according to the colours adjacent to it and also to colours some distance from it. The recommended procedures for painting simplified areas which are in colour relationships are described in the commentary to Pictures 109, 110 and 111.

When modelling in colour a watermelon or football, for example, it is necessary to capture the light, semi-shade and shadow. In this way the painted shape does not remain flat but gives an impression of space — of 'roundness'.

Children are aware that white will lighten any colour whereas black will darken it. However, this is a rather simplistic approach.

113 *Footballs I.* These round shapes are modelled in many variations of colours (bright and non-bright, light and dark). Painting in thick tempera enabled the children to put layers of paint on drying surfaces and thus emphasise the 'roundness of footballs' in colour contrasts. The children commented on their work in the following way: 'dark green at the front, light yellow at the back, light green at the front,' etc. They 'stroked' the rounded shapes

B Reznickova

114

of the footballs. They applied a brush dipped in water to larger surfaces where the shapes did not 'bounce off' each other.

114 *Footballs II.* This picture is less bright because the covering paints were diluted with water. A whole scale of cool blue shades and warm red shades was used in rendering the light. As in the previous picture, it is possible to observe (or even point to) the regular arrangement of the light and dark colours at the boundaries of shapes. These boundaries are also dividing lines between cool and warm colours. Left: This picture painted by a younger child can be used as a comparison. *Shiny Apples in a Basket* was painted only in local colours. The white suggests the sheen of the fruit. The apples are flat, not modelled using colour.

For example, where the light falls on a tomato it will become sweetly pink by adding white. It might be useful for children to try to model the 'roundness' of a football by using different colours. Pictures 113 and 114 show that the children did not want their footballs to be merely flat red coloured circles, so they differentiated the shadows on the balls by using colder blue-greens or green-browns, and also darker shades of a warmer red-violet colour. They chose diluted weak colours, even the lightest yellow and orange, for the surfaces on which the light fell. To make the footballs really round they had to paint the background as well. However, the ball's shape was not lost against it. Its lighter and warmer parts stood out better against the dark, cold background and its darker parts were not lost against the lighter background. For this exercise the children had to use their imagination but also closely observe contrasts of warmth and light.

115

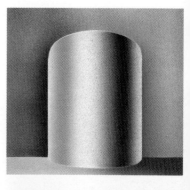

These Instructional Illustrations recall the contrasts used when painting cylindrical shapes. The first picture involves lightening the colour using white and darkening the colour using black. In the second picture black and white are not used. The shape is simply modelled by colour. Remember that yellow-orange and yellow-green are considered to be the light colours and blue, blue-violet and blue-green are the dark colours.

It takes a lot of time and practice to be able to see changes of contrast when painting a still life. It would not, however, be wise to ask children to spend an excessively long time on learning the minutiae of the painter's craft. An exact study of a model would extinguish that delightful childish quality which is so individual, even if it is at times naive. We should never try to impose our own vision of a still life on children. This would deprive them of the enjoyment of making discoveries through their own vision, an enjoyment which is

115 *Granny's Earthenware Jar.* This jar stood on a red tablecloth against a blue background. It was positioned at the height of the child's eyes to make the shape appear simple and undistorted, and enable the child to concentrate on portraying the light, semishade and shadow. The shades of brown were mixed with yellow and white. Black was also added in places where the light did not fall. The jar is in warmth and light contrast with both the background and the base.

116 *Still Life with Rounded Shapes and Edged Shapes.* This is the first stage of painting with diluted covering paints. The painter, a girl, first drew the basic outlines in charcoal and then marked the colour and light ratios for the entire still life. If we compare this first stage with the completed Picture 117, we can see that the ratios of colours, light and semi-shades remain unchanged.

116

intensified by the emotional links the children form. Younger children should be allowed to paint quite spontaneously — just place an interesting still life in front of them. Older children may be given some advice on the procedures described in the commentaries to Pictures 115, 116 and 117.

117

117 *Still Life.* The modelling was completed by adding colours and continually comparing them.

A *A Garden Still Life*. When your eyes get tired of looking at the bright colours of plants, you might welcome a chance to rest them by looking at the less bright colours of daily objects. Try to explore such objects with children.

B *An Old Phone Box* has suffered many wounds. Not every person manages to see the beauty of old objects whose paint is peeling.

C

C   *Unusual Bottles.* This art photograph shows the perfect arrangement and use of light in relation to three objects in primary colours. The bottles and the glass sphere are distinctively modelled by the light.

D   *A Shiny Orange.* The local colour of the orange is in fact the same everywhere. However, only half of it will shine in the bright light.

D

8

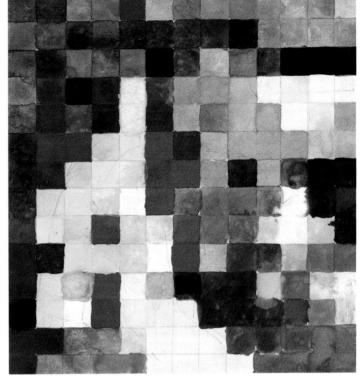

118 *The Random Counting of Colour Tones* from the oil painting *An Alley with Gallic-Roman Gravestones* (Les Alyscamps at Arles, 1888) by Paul Gauguin (1848–1903). This was painted in tempera, first in shades of green (on areas of similar size) and then in contrasting warm colours on smaller areas. The black accent in the centre indicates a group of mysterious figures from Gauguin's painting. Brushstrokes suggest the painter's regular tremulous style.

119 *Observing the Structure of a Painting Composed from Colour Contrasts* is based on the oil painting *The Boy in a Red Waistcoat* by Paul Cezanne (1839–1906). A girl painted a net of squares with covering paints. She tried to guess which colour tones the painter had used in a particular place. By alternating colours in gradually drying squares she was able to discover a part of the great secret of 'the father of modern painting'. Paul Cezanne would place surfaces of light warm colours and cool dark colours next to each other. The warmer colour seems closer to the observer and the painter used this to model the space gradually by alternating warm and cool colour tones.

Colour Messages from Painters

How to discuss painting. The key to sorting colour messages. 'Paraphrasing' adventures. The wild drama of colours, or the serene construction of a painting?

We keep the more demanding explanations of movements in painting for older children. However, we can start preparing the ground for a deeper appreciation and ultimately an understanding of paintings in younger children if we take them regularly to art galleries and painting exhibitions. There we can talk about paintings and their reproductions; ask questions of the children; and finally encourage them to paint from memory the picture they liked the most. 'Paraphrase' is the term used for such an imaginative

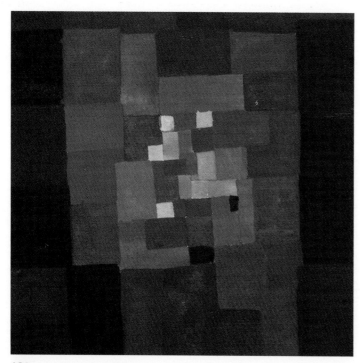

120

120 *Inspiration with the Discovery of Chiaroscuro* as seen in the painting called *Saskia* by Rembrandt Harmenszoon van Rijn (1606—69). A striking contrast of light and shade was revealed in simplified colour ratios. This management of light and shade, called chiaroscuro in Italian, was used by the Baroque painters.

121 *Spring Colours* in a painting by the Czech painter Jan Preisler (1872—1918). An older boy tried to record this in coloured blocks. He had a reproduction of the painting at his disposal for only a limited period of time, so he made notes on the symbolic use of colours: 'mysterious, shy grey-silver to pink; grey greens — suggesting allure, expectations and desire'.

121

122 *The Number of Colours Discovered in a Painting.* A child observed the reproduction of a painting and copied the colours in paint onto a sheet of paper. He later cut these out and arranged them in a scale of colours. An interesting game can follow if the cutout surfaces are then matched with colour samples from the reproduction.

123 *A Moving Impression* was evoked by the colours in *A Discourse in Provence* (1912–13) by Pierre Bonnard (1867–1947). An older boy recorded his observation with rapid brushstrokes. The sunshine made all the colours come alive; they sparkle and glitter, shimmer and flicker; the solid shapes of objects seem to submerge into them. The Impressionists were the first to try to render the world through rapid painting of coloured spots of light. Pierre Bonnard, a Post-Impressionist, added brightness to the colours.

123

124

124 *The Colours on Pierre Bonnard's Palette.* The children tried to determine this through the colours on a sheet of paper. They then cut the colours out and arranged them in a scale of warm and cool tones.

exercise; the expression of an experience. It is definitely not an attempt to copy a work of art. 'Paraphrasing' is a suitable activity for children. It helps them recall and experience the unique message from the painter more intensely.

After visiting a gallery several times, children can have their painted recollections before them simply by hanging a piece of string in their room and attaching their paintings to it with paper clips or clothes pegs. The child will then know that he has met Marc Chagall or Vincent van Gogh.

When we talk about reproductions of paintings, which can be easily obtained from magazines, calendars, exhibition catalogues or postcards, we might find a piece of string useful too. We should have at our disposal at least two or three reproductions of Renaissance, Baroque and Romantic paintings and perhaps more Impressionist reproductions. Our collection from the turn of the century could contain reproductions of works by Paul Cezanne, Paul Gauguin, Vincent van Gogh, Henri Matisse and Edward Munch.

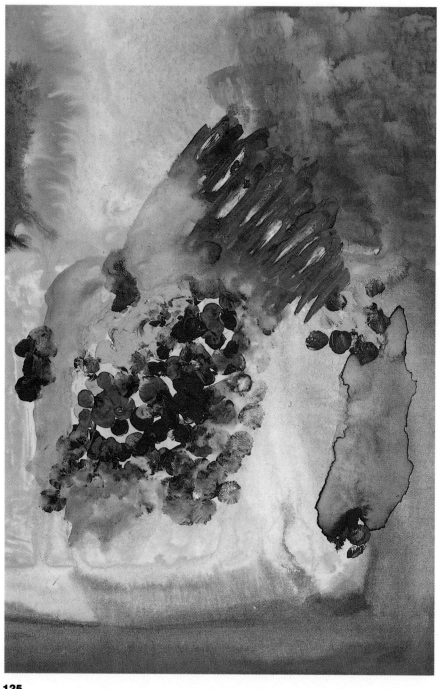

125

125 *Colours Remembered* from *Circus* (Circus Rider) by Marc Chagall (1887—1985). A girl selected the reproduction she liked best. She looked at it for a long time and then painted her colour impression of the painting in well-diluted colours on a wet surface. When she had completed the basic surfaces she looked at the reproduction once more and made her painting more accurate by adding tiny sparkling accents of bright colours. The colours on Chagall's painting are used expressively and emotionally. They make a statement of moods and memories.

Children will undoubtedly find the more modern painters such as Marc Chagall, Wassily Kandinsky, Joan Miro, Paul Klee and Pablo Picasso interesting. Modern art galleries or an encyclopedia of painting will provide inspiration when selecting the latest modern paintings. Remember that the selected reproductions should not include only objective paintings — portraits, still lifes and landscape

126

126 *Catching Mysterious Fish* with the painter Paul Klee (1879—1940). The children were interested in a reproduction of the oil painting entitled *Golden Fish*. Fish swim in the mysterious depths of an ocean. What are they talking about? Which fish is the most beautiful? One child painted his impression of the painting. His mysterious fish seems to be saying something; to be singing or perhaps even calling for help. The fish's mouth is expressively and symbolically marked with the colour red. This painting is a rather imaginative 'paraphrase' of the original painting, influenced by the topic itself and its mysterious surroundings.

127 *Paraphrases of 'Improvisation No. 30'* by Wassily Kandinsky (1866 to 1944). The children had seen several of Kandinsky's paintings. They gave their impressions of this painting as a vivid musical rhythm or movement. They were quite correct to do so. Some abstract painters did express movement, sound or music in their paintings. They associated their images with definite colouring, linear and shape rhythms.

— but abstract paintings too. Even as few as three reproductions is enough to begin.

Children can sort out, compare or select coloured reproductions according to certain criteria. They can try to get an understanding of a picture based on their own subjective feelings. After discussion they can attempt their own 'paraphrase' of a work of art.

127

128

128 *Wild Landscape* as remembered from a reproduction of *The Village Green* by Karl Schmidt-Rottluff (1884—1976). This is accompanied by the following commentary: 'It is painted in bright pure colours and lines by a person who would not allow himself to be laughed at.' Some German Expressionists did understand their paintings as huge coloured linear dramas.

A game involving reproductions can be quite simple. Children first attach portraits, then still lifes and finally landscapes onto a piece of string. They also place abstract paintings on a table and try to describe their feelings; whether the painting reminds them of a movement, a dance, music, secret writing, a warning or whether it evokes happiness or sadness.

In the next stage of the game, children will retain only those paintings which they like best. The reason for selection might be that a painting is full of colour and its shapes evoke happiness; or that it is the most vivid or dramatic. The children can then be asked to provide reasons for selecting a particular painting. By talking about a picture, children will gradually discover the means of expression used by the painter — whether it is marked colour contrasts, paste painting or dominant rich and bright tones.

Paintings can also be compared with each other by asking such questions as: Which of the paintings is the most vivid? Where can you see the greatest contrast of light and shadow? Where was line used as a means of expression? The questions do not have to concern only the means of expression. Other possible questions are: Which painting would you like to be part of in a dream? Can you describe the landscape in this painting as if you were wandering about in it? What would you say to the figures in these paintings?

129 a) 'A flower girl with daisies who is well sun-tanned.'

b) 'To be noticed by people a flower girl should have flowers in her hair; she should shout loudly and offer her flowers for sale to passers-by.'

c) 'A flower girl moves like a ballet dancer; she has a fulfilling job.'

Younger children painted these three pictures after seeing *The Flower Girl* (right) by Czech painter Josef Čapek (1887—1945). The children were allowed to ascertain the position of the Flower Girl by tracing the fundamental lines onto thinner paper. They then painted their own variations of the painting and wrote commentaries on what the girl was doing. The words of Josef Čapek himself are an example of his involvement in expressive, emotional painting: 'One has to have a picture firmly imprinted in the heart in order to fill the eyes with it later.'

129   a   b   c

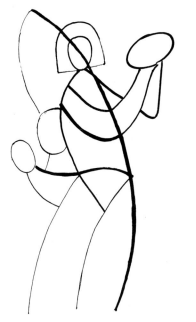

Understanding the colour messages from painters is linked in many respects to what was discussed in the previous chapters. For example, tell children to attach the reproductions with predominant shades of warm colours to the string on the right hand side of the room and the reproductions with predominant cold shades to the string on the left. Or tell them to count up how many tones of blue, including blue-green and blue-violet shades, are in a particular painting. Can they mix these blue tones on a palette? They may discover a colour accent in painting, which does not disappear even when they close their eyes.

Children can also try to give titles to paintings according to any significant details or predominant colours (such as 'A Blue Landscape with a Red House'). They might also be able to determine which ones were painted outside, ones in which the painter attempted to capture changing reality with several quick brush-

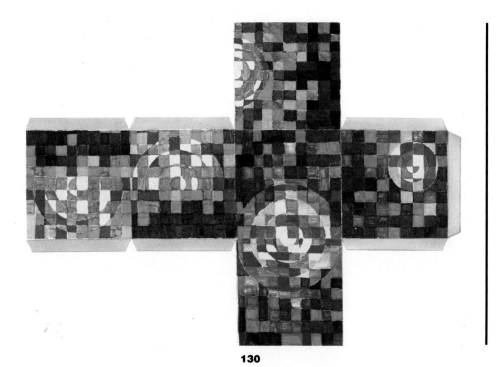

130

130 *A Colour Composition of the Six Sides of a Cube.* This topic is suitable for older children. First, the children drew and cut out the cube's covering. Then they drew a linear division of nets connecting across the cube's edges. They coloured small surfaces in felt-tip pens, arranging the colours from warm to cold.

131 a

b

c

131 a), b), c) *Greetings to Victor Vasarely* or Rubik's Cubes which revolve on their own. The children observed the paintings of Victor Vasarely (b. 1908) who constructed colours in geometrical nets in such a manner that they evoked an impression of movement, falling, curving or rotating. The children tried to create their own puzzle — a cube which might deceive the human eye in the same way as the work of op-artists. The Hungarian painter Victor Vasarely collaborated with Erne Rubik in designing the artistic form of his puzzles.

strokes. Children can differentiate between paintings in which the artist conveys feelings and moods and paintings which are intellectual reflections and remind us of colour structures.

At the end of any sorting activity, help the children to arrange the paintings in chronological order, according to their date of origin. Younger children do not have a clear concept of time so compare the date of a painting with a grandfather's birthday or with the notion of 'how old the painting might be'.

Altering a reproduction is usually good fun. If children place a mirror's edge upright to a painting then the colours will multiply along its axis. The painting can also be altered slightly by placing tiny pieces of coloured paper on the reproduction while observing changes in the original colour. It is possible to discover interesting details using a viewfinder. Further possibilities are described in the commentaries under this chapter's illustrations.

All the activities and discussions connected with the works of painters should start and end with a searching inner dialogue during which the spectator stands alone in front of the painting.

A

A Karl Schmidt-Rottluff, *The Village Green*. You can compare a reproduction of this painting with its 'paraphrase' in Picture 128. The colour in this painting has an expressive, emotional function. Not even the sun could colour the landscape so intensely. The Expressionist painter uses deliberately bright pure colours throughout the entire painting.

B

B *A Coloured Reconstruction of a Bird* is the work of an older boy. The bird's appearance, only preserved in the beak, is expressed as a triangular pyramid. The eyes and geometrically arranged feathers are constructed on the pyramid. In this instance the colour is part of the entire design.

C Victor Vasarely, *Tupa — 2, 1972*, serigraph (93 x 80 cm). The children felt like touching this painting's reproduction because the illusion of space, geometrically constructed by the artist, was so lifelike. Vasarely referred to his work as 'l'unité plastique' (the plastic unity of colour and shape). If you observe the change of shape you will also notice a change of colour. The painter's work includes an incredible number of colour gradations and shape variations.

132

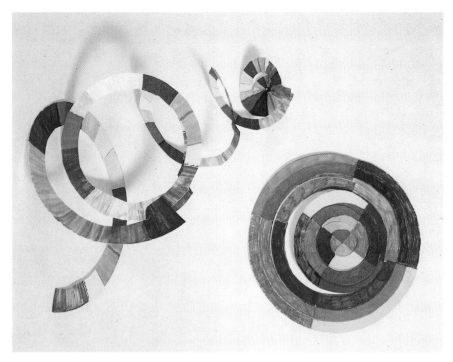

133

9

132 *Op-art's Mobile Puzzles.* Six children designed a school wall panel consisting of six grey squares. The original panel was composed of twelve squares. The children were inspired by the movement of a coloured windmill. If we imagine the parts unfolded then we would have in front of us three squares and three circles. The children coloured these with felt-tip pens using the contrast of warm and cool colours with accents of light. They then cut them into circular or angular sections, and fitted and glued them together.

33 *A Rotating Coloured Windmill.* A younger child designed this paper model. First, he coloured a circle with felt-tip pens in different warm colours. He cut the circle in a spiral. When he put weight in the centre, the spiral rotated beautifully from the third level to the ground level. It looked good when it was hung or shaped by folding. It could also be suspended in a children's playground.

Colour and Environment

Applied art. Toy designs. Coloured habitats. Decorative walls for nursery schools and department stores. Links between shape and motifs. Colour changes of a room.

Architects and designers shape the environment in which we live. They design houses, furniture, glass, ceramics, textiles, clothes and even car bodies. They need to have not only great imagination but also a feel for the material with which they work, and for shape, colour and precise finishing. Therefore, it may seem rather bold to attempt the work of professionals by trying architectonic designs and projects with children. However, some architects and designers are indeed interested in what climbing frames and chutes, sports clothing, toys or habitats the children themselves would de-

134 a   **b**

sign. It can assist them in ascertaining the environment in which people feel most at home.

Children can design toys using easily accessible materials. Pile up large and small plastic bottles and shampoo and cream containers in front of them and add old coloured socks, gloves, tights and a handful of buttons. By dressing up the bottles and changing their colour, the children can create fantastic figures and animals. Stuffed gloves make either hands or wings, buttons can serve as eyes. Individual parts of a body can then be sewn together and the figure hung on a piece of string. Typically, toys have big heads, distinctive eyes and bright colouring.

Toys can also be created by folding paper. Japanese 'origami' can serve as an inspiration. How interesting it would be for two children to fold a huge two-metre-high steamboat out of glued sheets of paper. They can later paint it. Various toys which can be suspended (Pictures 134, 135) are also worth experimenting with.

c

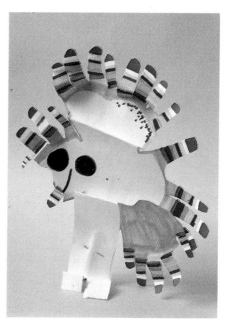

d

134 a) *A Happy Kite,* b) *A Bat-like Butterfly,* c) *A Duck Scarecrow,* d) *A Long-needled Bugaboo.* The shapes of these paper toys were created by tracing the children's fingers and then folding the paper. The children designed these toys as small kinetic sculptures.

If children fix a piece of wood to them they can then march these two-dimensional puppets up and down on an improvised stage. Three-dimensional paper toys can become more permanent features of the child's bedroom if we glue a timetable or a calendar onto

135

135 *A Goblin Catcher.* This design for a two-dimensional sculpture for a children's playground was created from a folded sheet of paper. When it was cut out, the figure was coloured with felt-tip pens and pieces of coloured paper were glued onto it. The goblin could catch coloured circles with his hands, horns and ears.

136

137

them. If a huge paper box is made into a toy it can serve as a target or a net for throwing balls in the garden or playground.

From an early age children like to build houses out of building blocks. It may occasionally seem that the common red-yellow-blue colours of building blocks cannot fully develop children's sense of colour. Pictures 136 and 137 show how boldly the children played with the images of other coloured environments. They enlivened black and white reproductions of housing estates and industrial sites with colour and shape. Some children enlarged their designs and painted into pre-constructed linear nets, as in Picture 138. The children also observed works by the Austrian architect and painter Fritz Hundertwasser (b. 1928) and photographs of fairy-like buildings by the Spanish architect Antonio Gaudí (1852–1926). Archi-

136 *Joining the Old and New Part of the Town in Colour.* An older boy used felt-tip pens to colour a magazine picture. In his commentary he explained that the town changed at night by switching on coloured spotlights.

137 *Grey Cement Works in Colour.* A girl used felt-tip pens to colour a magazine picture. Cement works covered in grey dust which pollutes the landscape magically changed into a pleasing environment in which to work. It reminds us of coloured beehives or children's toys.

138 *A Fantastic Skyscraper.* This work was inspired by a class visit to an exhibition of paintings and designs by the Austrian painter and designer Fritz Hundertwasser. The child who made this tempera painting first created a linear blue and red structure using a brush (below). He then composed colours (warm and cool in contrast) similar to stained glass.

tects' work is not only functional. We also experience the environment aesthetically and subjectively, especially when a building impresses us by its original design, charm, shape or colour.

Architecture is not only the external facade of buildings. If we enter a railway station, a restaurant or a department store, we notice what the interior is like, whether it is pleasant and attractive to the public. A work of art, a glass showcase, a mosaic or an adver-

138

117

139

140

139 *A Textile Shop Panel* was created as a collage from cut-up pieces of materials. The artist, a girl, balanced shapes and colours in an interesting structure. The panel windows suggest the simultaneous projection of a picture on several screens.

140 *An Advertisement for a Fashion Magazine* was also created as a collage. The author spent a long time shifting oblongs over the surface, finally deciding on the contrast of red oblongs against the light green of a skirt. The black accents provided background for the white lettering of the advertisement.

141 *An Advertising Board for a Shop or an Exhibition of Applied Glass* is also a collage. First, the oblong pictures of vases and glasses (in cool colours) were cut out of a magazine. The pictures were moved around for a long time until the colours and shapes became harmonious. Violet and grey colours remained in the centre; the edges had blue-green pieces of paper fixed to them.

141

tisement board can all go to make up interiors. They sometimes remind us of the function and role of the building through their design, topic or colour. We can encourage children to play designers: furnishing walls in a nursery, a music school, a fashion salon, a department store or a china shop.

Children should first realise that they are designing an enclosed whole — a square or an oblong. This has a bearing whether they are designing a panel using collage (Pictures 132, 139, 140, 141) or templates which are sprayed on or have paints spread over them (Pictures 142, 143, 145). Designers refer to the way in which a motif

142

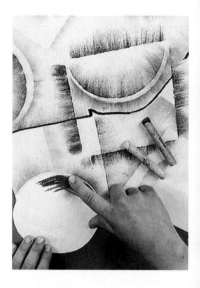

142 *A Blue Square.* An older boy designed this decorative panel. He first subdivided the white area by spreading dark chalks over the edges of square and circle templates. He then sprayed blue colours onto the whole area while using a piece of paper to cover parts of it. He also used red ink.

is linked to a given format. The motif (e.g. a violin or abstract geometric shape) cannot exceed the area, which is contrary to other activities in which children design textiles or wallpaper. The motif is 'placed', for example, into a square. It is simplified and two-

143

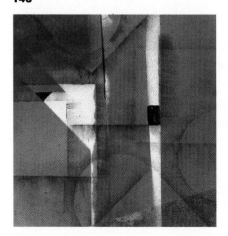

144

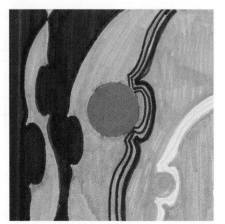

143 *A Red Square* was created in a similar way to Picture 142. However, this panel uses a pleasing contrast of olive green against raspberry red. The white areas, which contrast from a light point of view, are also designed sensitively. By turning the painting around the most appropriate position for the black accent was discovered. This black oblong in fact 'holds together' the entire square. Note that these works were created rapidly but further work on them could be more adventurous. An observer could be asked to choose only two of ten squares which he feels to be perfectly designed.

144 *A Square with Violin Shapes.* An older girl decided on an objective motif — a violin — for her design of a decorative panel. She imaginatively repeated the outline of a violin in different sizes on the square area. She selected warmer tones with contrasting light areas. She also used the two-dimensional contrast of a red circle to represent a music note and lines to remind us of musical notation. The picture is done with coloured felt-tip pens. If enlarged it would be suitable for an entrance hall to a music school.

145 *A Poster with Keys.* The children used parts of a subjective motif when designing the decorative area of this poster. Using a flat hard brush they spread a thick tempera paint over a template of a key. They toned the remaining areas of the background in warmer colours. Blue was the only colour used in contrast against the yellow area.

145

dimensional and its colours are based on multiple contrasting possibilities of light and warmth; a suitable accent will link the whole format optically.

There are many specialised publications and advertising brochures on home design (arrangement, colour and shape) and furnishings. Generally speaking, each house reveals something about the nature, preferences and tastes of its inhabitant. One

146

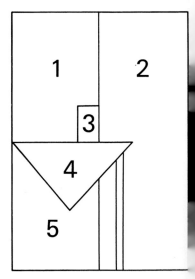

146 *Colour Changes of a Room.* A boy designed four colour variations using four schemes identical in shape. There could have been more·variations. Imagine gradual changes with the tablecloth being red, deep blue, white or brown.

a) A warm design for the room — light contrast

b) A contrasting design for the room — contrast of warm and cool colours

c) A cold design for the room — light contrast

d) A contrasting design for the room — using the contrast of a single deep yellow against reflected light greens.

Note that dark colours seem to make a space smaller; cold colours make a space cooler (a person is said to concentrate better in a room toned in cold colours). Light and warm colours have opposite optical effects. A bright environment is said to evoke a good mood.

1 Wall
2 Curtain
3 Vase
4 Table cloth
5 Carpet

might not feel so comfortable in a neighbour's house. When we stay in a hotel we might find the room's shape and colour design, no matter how perfect, rather impersonal. The child's bedroom does not have to be something resembling a storage room full of coloured objects. We should encourage children to think about their own rooms, and eventually to design their own model habitat. They could start by making 'a doll's living room' out of a cardboard box. A piece of material could represent the carpet, and children could

147 *A Playroom for Younger Children.* An older girl completed a black and white picture of a nursery school interior using coloured felt-tip pens. She added the following commentary: 'The blue walls will make the children's white-framed pictures stand out; blue reminds us of the sky. The brown floor reminds us of the earth, light-coloured toys can be neatly arranged on it. The drawers are of different colours to make identification easier — as in beehives. Certain toys are placed in each drawer. The surfaces of the low tables could be colour-coded with "play mats" — one with a green meadow, one with a desert, and one with a landscape including a road and a river. Children could place toys, animals, ships and other objects on these mats.'

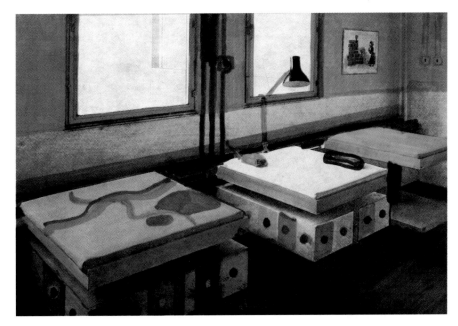

147

then choose suitable colours for walls, furniture (made out of matchboxes), curtains and a tablecloth. The children's illustrations provide further suggestions.

It would be wonderful if only sensitive art designers were responsible for the industrial production of daily objects, thus improving the public's perception and taste.

148

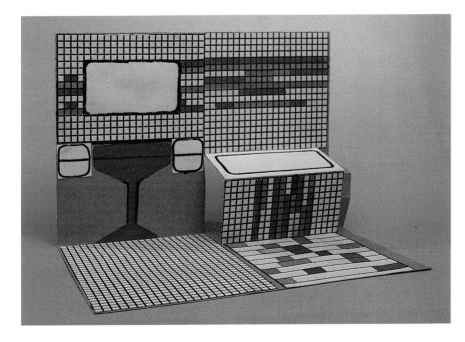

148 *The Bathroom.* Even very young children can design coloured variations for tiling compositions. A folded pastel-coloured sheet of paper can represent the bathroom wall and floor. A bathtub can emerge from the wall by making several incisions. Children can then glue on squares of paper representing tiles.

A Children love borrowing their mothers' clothes and trying out colour combinations of their own design.

A

B *Paint Your Own Sock.* This is an example of body art which encourages the painting of one's body. The origins of this art go back to the origins of beings.

B

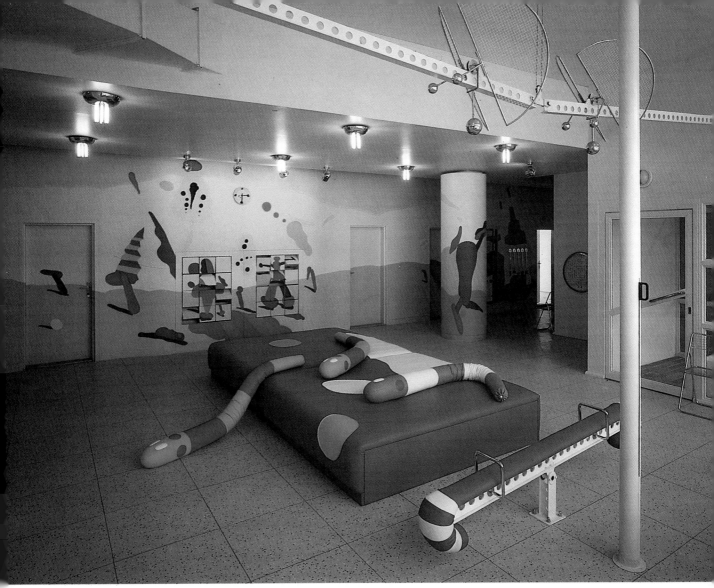

C Aleš Lamr, *The Interior of a Waiting Room in Prague's Health Centre for Children*, 1991. This is the third work by this painter in our book. The children appreciate the colour vitality and originality in his work. Aleš Lamr often collaborates with architects.

D *My Lips Are Zipped Up.* A part of this face is painted in a similiar fashion to the design of a jersey.

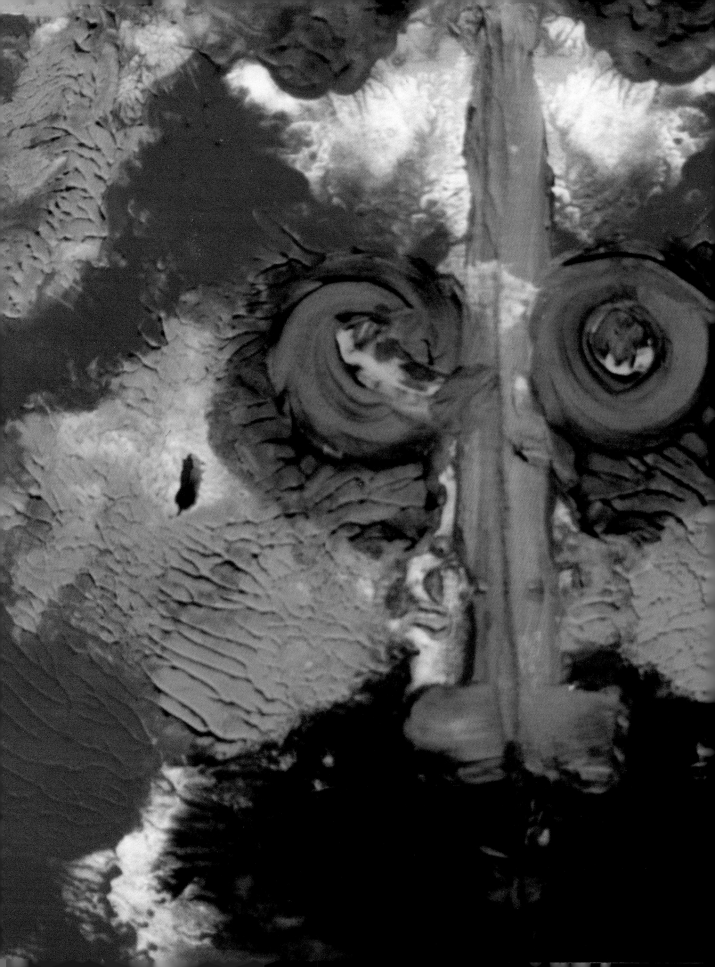